# SPECIAL NEEDS
# Special Families

# SPECIAL NEEDS

## Special Families

### BY AVIS COLEMAN

authorHOUSE®

*AuthorHouse™ LLC*
*1663 Liberty Drive*
*Bloomington, IN 47403*
*www.authorhouse.com*
*Phone: 1-800-839-8640*

*Published by AuthorHouse 02/11/2014*

*ISBN: 978-1-4918-6058-8 (sc)*
*ISBN: 978-1-4918-6057-1 (e)*

*Library of Congress Control Number: 2014902092*

# Table of Contents

# Special Families
## By Avis Coleman

## Introduction

When my dear friend (and fellow mother of five, Katrina Laygo) called and asked me to write for her new magazine, I was thrilled. I also felt apprehensive and unworthy of her noble project. This lovely lady had learned a year before that her fourth child, Nathan, was autistic. The shocking diagnosis sparked the advocate in Katrina and she began searching for ways to improve her child's quality of life and, hopefully, help others in the process. Her motivation was so sincere and inspiring, I felt humbled. She convinced me she needed me, and that was all it took. I began writing for *Something Special* Magazine, producing two to five feature stories per issue since its inception in 2009. Katrina never had to twist my arm because I have always had a soft spot in my heart for people with special needs/abilities. I grew up in a very small town and a tiny church community that was our family's second home. We were charter members of the church and my parents were very active. We knew and loved each and every family as if we were all related. One incredible family had a daughter named Debbie with Down syndrome. None of us knew that she was "different." She was just Debbie, and a part of our extended family.

When I began working for a television station after college, I covered a wide range of topics. But my favorite stories were always the "human interest" ones. Nothing made me feel more fulfilled than to write and produce a minute-plus-long segment about someone overcoming the odds. I also loved the opportunity to broadcast a need in the community (such as a burned-out family, a much-needed organ transplant or a struggling non-profit's cause). I rejoiced in the way Columbians and (soon after) Savannahians rallied to help.

When I was 32, I met the man of my dreams. At 35, I married John Coleman and we wasted no time before trying to have children. Each and every doctor we consulted drilled into my head that my age would be a factor in conceiving a child. I was told my chances of a high-risk pregnancy and birth defect rose exponentially each and every year. After several years of unsuccessful efforts, we finally decided on invitro; I was 39. God blessed us with beautiful and healthy twins and we thought we'd met our blessings quota. But two years later, our handsome Aidan arrived. Fourteen months after that, the adorable Brendan joined our family and then, when I was 43 years old, we learned that number five was on the way. By this time, we knew our luck was running short and doctors all but begged us to have amniocentesis. We wouldn't hear of it. At nine weeks, we did undergo the alpha feta protein (AFP) test, which came back terribly suspicious. We were told that, based on the lab results, we had a one-in-four chance of Down syndrome and that we were actually at a much higher risk when my age was factored in. After about 20 minutes spent digesting this information, my husband looked at me and said, "Well, if that's how it goes, you'll be the best Special Olympics mom anyone's ever seen!" Our precious

1

little spitfire, Grace, was born that summer as healthy and perfect as any child can be. We will never know what we did to deserve these incredible children, but we are very thankful we did it.

Another *very special* child came into our world thanks to my brother-in-law. Stephen Coleman (now five) was diagnosed with cerebral palsy much sooner than many of us were willing to believe and certainly before we were able to accept it. His story is later on in this book. He brings so much joy and so many laughs to family get-togethers. I can't stop kissing him and hugging him and he gets quite tired of me. Eventually, he starts saying in his precious baby voice, "Bye, bye Avis" to get rid of me. I often wonder if he thinks that's my name.

Every story I have written for the magazine has brought tears of joy, and sometimes sorrow, to the families and this empathetic writer. I am now friends on Facebook with many of the parents I have interviewed. We commiserate and we celebrate everything from children's events to political nonsense. I thank my Lord every day for many things. The ability to write and share the stories of these strong, vibrant families is something I take very seriously. The articles you find in this book have already graced *Something Special* Magazine. They represent a compilation of my features from the first two years. You will also notice that I added an update after each feature since (for too many reasons to mention) it has taken me two years to bring this book to completion. The journalist in me couldn't tell their stories without letting you know what has occurred in their lives since the articles were originally published.

I hope you enjoy reading about some of *the most special people* I have had the pleasure to meet. I hope you find their lives and their dedication inspiring. We'll begin with Daniel's story:

# 105 Surgeries and Counting

### Daniel Deloach

It was the first of hundreds of tumors Julia Deloach would see in her soon-to-be born son, Daniel. She was five months pregnant when her gut instinct told her she needed an ultrasound. Her third child felt bigger than he was supposed to be and a creeping suspicion had been gnawing at her that something was wrong. She asked her husband, Michael, to go with her to the hospital, "thinking that my whole life was about to change," remembers Julia. She was right. Her five-month-old fetus had a large tumor, about one third the size of his abdomen. The Deloaches were sent to Augusta the next day for an amniocentesis, which showed no genetic abnormalities but the ultrasound showed a clear malformation on the tiny baby's body. The doctors recommended abortion.

"I told them I wouldn't even talk about it," said Julia. "Whatever is wrong, we'll deal with it." And that was the beginning of Julia and Michael Deloach's journey with their amazing son.

Daniel's sister, Kathleen, was four years old and his brother, Michael, wasn't yet 18 months when the Deloaches were told he has Proteus Syndrome. This condition gained notoriety after Joseph Merrick, known as the "Elephant Man," was diagnosed with PS in 1987. There is a film based on the tragic life of Merrick, who suffered both physically and emotionally from his condition and the humiliating ridicule of the people he encountered.

There are varying degrees of severity and differing affects of Proteus. Daniel's condition has manifested as prolific tumors, giantism of the feet and hemi-hypertrophy (where one part of the body grows faster and bigger than the other). His beautiful face and bright smile seldom reflect any of the pain and struggle of the 105 surgeries he has endured. His cheerful disposition and positive approach to life are a testament to his own inner strength. He is an inspiration to others. He gives credit for his success to his family, united in their love and support of him.

## DANIEL'S STORY:

"There's a big pocket of fluid on his back, the size of a grapefruit," Julia recalls the doctor's words after viewing Daniel's first ultrasound. But there was nothing they could do but wait. Until he was born, the family didn't know what to expect or what was in store for them. Daniel entered the world following a six-hour Caesarean Section at Memorial Health University Hospital. The delivery was touch-and-go with doctors cautiously avoiding his tumors to avoid any trauma to his fragile little body. Daniel weighed in at 13 pounds with a questionable Apgar score. Julia was whisked away to the recovery room where she began asking to see her baby. She was not allowed to see him.

"The doctor came in and told us she didn't think Daniel would ever walk," recalls Julia.

Michael responded much the same way he would for the next 23 years. "It's going to be OK," he told his wife. "We'll do this together."

They brought Daniel home from the hospital for about a week, then Julia again sensed something was wrong. She didn't like the way his breathing sounded. Daniel's parents put him in his car seat for the trip to Augusta but quickly took him out because his breathing was so irregular. When they arrived at the Medical College of Georgia emergency room, doctors found that his tumor had grown. He was bleeding into the tumors. His hemoglobin was at a frighteningly low 5, down from 11 just the week before. Julia was convinced if she hadn't taken him out of that seat, he wouldn't have survived the ride because he had lost so much blood. Emergency room doctors had to slice Daniel's four limbs trying to get to his veins before finally running a central line straight into his chest.

Michael Sr. returned home two days later to get Kathleen and Michael because he and Julia wanted their older children with them to tackle Daniel's medical battles as a family. This became a way of life for the Deloach family for years to come.

While Michael was making the trip to Savannah for the other children, a well-respected geneticist, Dr. David Flannery, stopped Julia in the hallway of the hospital to offer his theory on Daniel's condition. It was the first time anyone had suggested Proteus Syndrome.

Dr. Charles Howell, a doctor who would take care of Daniel for the next two years, told the Deloaches with tears in his eyes that he would do the best he could. The next day he operated on Daniel, removing the large tumor. But the ordeal wasn't over. The incision became infected and the family stayed in Augusta for nine more surgeries over the next three to four weeks. While there, Daniel started spiking a high fever, his white blood cell count was up to 30,000 and Julia "started acting like a medical technologist, sneaking around to get the blood test results" and convinced Dr. Howell that there was another infection. She was right. Dr. Howell credited Julia with saving Daniel's life again as they removed the contaminated central line.

Daniel survived his many surgeries and continued to grow. When he was 2, Dr. Howell recommended that he see an orthopedist. His feet were enlarged and they grew pointing backward. His next surgery involved breaking his legs and turning his feet. He wore a full body cast at that time, and wore another at 4 and still another at 6, for spinal column correction. "Mike would tell Daniel, 'you owe me a thousand hiney wipes.' We're getting older and closer to Daniel paying up," Julia laughs.

The hardest and most frightening surgeries were the ones around the spinal cord. The doctor had to fuse it with a rod to get the tumor out. There was always the fear of damage to the spinal cord and the effects of such damage. He had three of these operations.

Another frightening development happened recently when one of his kidneys began bleeding for no apparent reason. He had a vascular malfunction that had imploded the kidney and the entire organ had to be removed.

Daniel has endured at least 105 surgeries. By the time he hit 50 of them, his mother had put him on a local swim team along with Kathleen and Michael. She felt it was the only sport he could enjoy safely and it gave him strong swimming skills. After his 100th surgery at age 20, the family threw a celebration party that combined Daniel's milestone with Michael's graduation from the U.S. Naval Academy.

Throughout each series of surgery, rehabilitation and therapy, the family stuck together and pulled each other through. Julia recalls that prior to their many trips to Augusta for surgery, the children would often drive there together the day before to get Daniel's blood drawn. There weren't many cell phones at that time and Julia would worry about being on the highway with three young children. Kathleen would inevitably set the mood, often singing sweet church songs, "One that she would sing, 'Here I am Lord,' would almost bring me to tears," recalls Julia. Kathleen was always nervous before Daniel's surgeries, throwing up from nerves and worrying because she knew Mommy wasn't coming back home with them for a while. Julia had to stay with Daniel. "It was heart wrenching, needing and wanting to stay with Daniel. I wouldn't leave my baby alone," recalls Julia. "But there were two other tiny people who needed me too. Mike said they would cry the whole way home after leaving us at the hospital." While at the hospital with Daniel, Julia would spend lots of time on the phone staying connected. Whenever possible, it was her goal to keep the family together.

Proteus Syndrome affected all their lives. And it affected them in some positive ways.

Twenty-three years later, Julia's persistence has paid off. All three of her children have turned out strong, accomplished and devoted to family. Their childhood experiences have made them compassionate, focused and faith-centered.

Kathleen graduated with honors from Furman University with an undergraduate degree in political science and communications and earned a master's degree in Bioethics at Case Western Reserve University in Cleveland. She recently earned her Ph.D. in public health, is a professor at Armstrong Atlantic, a bio-ethicist at St. Joseph's/Candler, and has written a book called *Daniel's World* to help children understand others with disabilities or differences. Michael graduated from Naval Academy among the top 50 in a class of a 1,000. He's a Junior Lieutenant in a Riverine Squadron of the Navy, about to be deployed to Iraq. Kathleen married John Rex Benton who told Kathleen he was amazed at the family strength, "I had no idea what you all have gone through all your life,'" Kathleen recalls Rex saying to her.

Once, during Kathleen's dating years, Daniel called his sister to tell him about a major surgery coming up. "She was on a date with this dude," Daniel remembers. "But she left and came to see me."

Recently, when Daniel's kidney ordeal was threatening, his brother Michael began working on a plan to get to Savannah and be with Daniel through the surgery. Michael was out on a training mission. Kathleen called and heard machine guns in the background. Michael, choking back tears, said he would leave that afternoon. He called for a ride, stood on a small Virginia street corner until his cousin arrived, traveled through the night and was in Savannah at 6 a.m. to be with Daniel. "God had a hand in that visit," said Julia. A snowstorm in Virginia gave Michael the opportunity to stay a few more days. He didn't want to leave until his brother was off the respirator. The next day at 4 a.m., Daniel pulled it out himself and Michael got back on the road to return to the base. "It's unbelievable," says Julia of her children. "They're so giving. It's hard to describe how much they love each other."

Daniel has had that kind of effect on every life he's touched. He's made friends and has followers from all aspects of his life; from his early days at Blessed Sacrament School, to Benedictine Military Academy to his friends and professors at SCAD, as well. Professor Joel Varland told Julia, "he has had every right to be bitter, mad, mean and angry, but instead he brings so much life and passion to my classroom."

The happy, well-adjusted young man has overcome many obstacles during the course of his life. His parents' tenacity taught him at a very young age to be comfortable in his own skin in spite of his condition. Putting him on a swim team took guts. "Growing up I didn't like people staring at me," said Daniel. "And here I was in a bathing suit with everything exposed. That Speedo showed every scar and bump and it was hard to get up there in front of everyone. I never won because I didn't have the endurance. I always came in last place. That was hard, busting it and never winning. Well, there was one race I got first place. I still have the ribbon. Out of four people, I got first place."

The stares, the finger pointing and the mean-spirited comments were always a part of Daniel's life and he learned to live with the reactions of others. His siblings and friends, however, never could accept the rudeness of strangers. One BSS friend was sent to the principal's office for punching someone who'd made fun of Daniel. Some BC buddies "bushed" a fellow for saying something insulting to Daniel. Michael and Kathleen learned, grudgingly, to take it—just like Daniel did. "I went to a Proteus Syndrome conference when I was 12," recalls Daniel. "I told the kids it will get better. I told them kids can be mean and ignorant. They don't think about what they're saying and doing. My family never ever let me feel sorry for myself. They said, 'if people are looking at you, tell them that's how God made you.'"

And God made Daniel strong enough to survive the surgeries—even the most painful of them—and come out with that smile on his face. The recent kidney surgery was among the most difficult of them all. "When they removed the kidney, there was so much pressure from the blood, it literally imploded," recalls Daniel. "I saw the doctor when I came out of the coma, and he said, 'Daniel, I gave you a 20 percent chance of living.'"

It's easy to be in awe of Daniel and his courage, his strength and his spunk. It isn't easy to imagine his suffering. "Most people who meet him don't realize what he's been through, especially all the operations," says Michael Sr. proudly. "The part they don't see is that he wakes up every morning and throws up. That's how he starts his day. He's constantly nauseous. And those are the good days when that's all he's dealing with. But he carries (his burden) well. He's just remarkable to me. I'm his father, not to brag but I could never do what he's done."

It's not just Daniel's ability to cope with Proteus Syndrome that makes him impressive but, it's also his unbelievable talent that dazzles those who know him. His meticulous acrylic paintings are stunning; and on par with many of the masters. He has a keen culinary sense and enjoys creating exquisite meals with his organic meats and vegetables and he's majoring in Industrial Design at the Savannah College of Art and Design where he'll put his artistic talents to practical use one day. "My goal is to finish SCAD, get my industrial design degree, design medical equipment and household tools," says Daniel. "I want to redesign bandages, redesign scissors and scalpels. My other dream is to write a book called *The Professional Patient*. It is going to be a handbook for doctors, nurses and health care specialists. It will be a 'what to do and what not to do' kind of book."

One thing Daniel says we are not to do is take life for granted. Michael recalls a phone call from his son, "He called me one night and said, 'Dad, I don't want you think you aren't a good dad. You're the best dad I could ever have.' Daniel really does keep life in perspective," says Michael. "I know life is hard for him and he has troubles. Now that he's out in the world, he expects everybody to be his friend but it's hard for people to warm up to him. But he handles it well. I don't know how he does it. He is remarkable. Whatever problems I have, they don't even begin to amount to what he faces."

Daniel will tell you in a heartbeat that he owes it all to his supportive, wonderful family: "If I were to meet up with God, and He said I could start my life over with a normal body but with a different family *or* He said I could have the *same* family but have Proteus, I swear I would pick Proteus Syndrome because of the effect they had on me and the effect I have had on them."

Two months ago, when Daniel was facing that potentially fatal kidney failure, he told his mother to be strong for Kathleen and Michael if something happened to him. "I realized that day, I have strength because I still have my child," Julia says. "We will fight every battle. I have a lot of Faith. Through everything, God's been pretty good to me. I can always find that silver lining. I can always see His divine intervention. God has always come through for me." And for Daniel.

## TWO YEARS LATER

Daniel continues to smile and light up a room in spite of his condition. In 2011, Daniel lost his right kidney. This past June, he was diagnosed with Pulmonary Hypertension but it turned out a tumor was invading the pleural cavity. He is currently on a Trilogy at night and on oxygen 24/7. He is on an experimental drug called Rapamycin to, prayerfully, shrink the tumor. His sister, Kathleen and her husband, Rex, have two beautiful children, Julia Grace (3) and Jack (1) who this author thinks looks just like Daniel. Brother Michael married Sarah Eve in November and is currently getting his US Navy Masters in National Security Middle Eastern and African Affairs.

# Friday the 13th
## Lauren Dotson's Story

You always know where you were when you found out something tragic happened. Bunny and Kevin Dotson can tell you exactly where they were when their life turned upside down. They remember the date like it was yesterday. It was Friday 13, 2004. That was the day they learned their precious 7-year-old daughter, Lauren, had a brain tumor.

Their saga began just a few days earlier on a typical Tuesday afternoon. Bunny had taken Lauren to the pediatrician's office for treatment of a foot condition. As an afterthought, Bunny mentioned to the physician's assistant that Lauren's balance was a little off. Lauren was given some drops and treated for a sinus condition. Then, on Thursday, Lauren's lack of equilibrium was so pronounced she had trouble walking on the bleachers at a basketball game. Bunny and Kevin knew then and there something was wrong.

On Friday the 13th, Bunny dropped off Lauren at school and watched her child literally wobble to the curb. Since she had to work that day, Bunny called the doctor's office and made an appointment. She called Kevin to pick Lauren up from school and take her. Bunny said she'd meet him there.

After a brief checkup and hearing a detailed description of Lauren's symptoms, Dr. Ramon Ramos told the Dotsons to go straight to the hospital and not to stop for lunch. Lauren was going to have a CT scan of her head. Bunny headed to school to pick up something for Lauren and to tell the second grade teacher, Collette Sego, what was going on (though she didn't know much at the time). With a heavy heart, Kevin did as he was instructed.

When Kevin and Lauren got to the hospital, the technicians immediately took Lauren back for her scan. Minutes later, the technician found Kevin and said the doctor needed to see him. He left his beloved child in the waiting room with a nurse. When he walked in that room, he knew. Dr. Ramos was waiting for him, apparently having left his office when Lauren and Kevin did so he could be at the hospital as soon as the scan was completed.

Dr. Ramos told Kevin there was a mass on Lauren's brain.

Lauren was admitted to the hospital. Bunny's voice falters as she recalls receiving that call from Kevin and he was crying. He told her the doctors had found something and she had to come immediately.

Bunny was at home when she got that call, and right away started arrangements for Lauren's brother, Ryan. Kevin's parents agreed to take care of Ryan and an army of family and friends helped maintain the duties at home. Ryan was 11 when his only sibling began her medical whirlwind.

Bunny was frantically trying to pack for herself and Lauren and pulling together Ryan's schedule for her in-laws. When she left her son that night to join Kevin and Lauren at the hospital, Bunny truly didn't know when she'd return and had no idea what was in store for her family. But a surprise visitor a few hours later provided the first hint that she wouldn't be alone in this journey. Lauren's teacher, Mrs. Sego, had stopped in at the hospital to offer support. It was there that Bunny and Kevin met with Dr. Ramos. He recommended a pediatric neurosurgeon named Timothy Mapstone at Egleston Hospital. In just a few hours since diagnosis, the Dotsons were heading to Atlanta and the battle of their lives.

After several hours on I-16 and I-75, they finally settled into their cozy little room on the fifth floor of Egleston. That's when the frenetic work of the staff began. They started medications to shrink the tumor until surgery. Lauren was pricked and prodded but in a way that wasn't terribly frightening for the little girl. She was a patient at a children's hospital where they'd done it all before.

The next morning, Dr. Mapstone came to explain Lauren's protocol. The surgery to remove the mass on her brain was scheduled for Tuesday. "Lauren knew she was sick and that's all," recalls Bunny. "She knew she had a 'boo boo' but didn't know where. She trusted us. She never had any questions."

Then, the amazing began to happen. Friends and family began arriving from Savannah. That hint of the support to come was blossoming into reality—the Dotsons weren't traveling this road alone. "Even her little girl friends were up there," Bunny says with a smile. "The girls played with Lauren in a little sitting room. And we had a fun dinner for them Monday afternoon in her room."

That same day, the Dotsons met someone who would become very important in their lives, their oncologist, Dr. Anna Janss. She was honest and straightforward. She said there would be a biopsy of the tumor once it was removed. She would let them know the results as soon as she had them. "To be honest, I didn't know how I could cope and do this," says Bunny. "You hear of this in other families but not mine. At that point we didn't know the outcome. We could only pray."

Tuesday morning arrived and Lauren was wheeled away for a surgery that lasted two and a half hours. Dr. Mapstone happily reported that the tumor was removed intact. They'd extracted every single bit of it. It hadn't metasthesized. She was "a good risk."

The results of the biopsy came in on Friday. The tumor was malignant. "It was so hard to grasp that my child had cancer." And a side effect they'd been warned about had occurred: after the surgery, Lauren couldn't talk.

The doctors had explained that a trauma to the brain (like this surgery) would almost certainly affect one's ability to communicate. It could be several weeks or even years before Lauren could talk again. But Lauren surprised her concerned parents just a few weeks later. "She couldn't even crack a smile," recalls Bunny. "It was strange the way it happened. Her aunt and uncle were there polishing her toes. Her uncle was rambling on to the unresponsive Lauren, telling her that he has to paint her aunt's toes 'because she can't reach them' and all of a sudden, Lauren started laughing. "It was the first sound we had heard from her in two and a half weeks!" laughs Bunny, remembering. "She started laughing out loud!"

Kevin had been going back and forth from Savannah to Atlanta on the weekends and wasn't there for the excitement. But they called him at once. Bunny told him, "Out of the blue, we were listening to a Martina McBride CD and she started laughing and *singing*!" Bunny held out the phone for Kevin to listen to this remarkable accomplishment. Then Lauren started talking. First it was "NNNNNNoooo" for yes, but by end of the day she was talking in complete sentences. Lauren started speech therapy that next day and was soon back to talking up a storm.

The Dotsons stayed at Egleston until March 10, when Lauren was transported to Scottish Rite for rehabilitation. The tumor and the surgery had left Lauren unable to walk. The left side of her body was dramatically weakened. They stayed at Scottish Rite for three and a half weeks undergoing occupational and physical therapy. While there, they had to be transported back and forth to Emory for radiation treatments to Lauren's head and spine. Dr. Janss determined that a combination of chemo and radiation was the best protocol and Lauren underwent 30 treatments of radiation for six weeks. "That was the worst part of the whole thing," says Bunny. "It made her sick and blah. We were told to give her whatever she wanted during this process. If she doesn't want to eat, don't force it. We were told not to talk to her if she doesn't want to talk."

She started her chemo treatments at Egleston, and after two rounds of treatment there, she was able to come home on March 24. She took the remainder of her treatments at Bacchus Children's Hospital. She would go in for overnight stays where she was given drip bags of three different kinds of chemo. She was carefully monitored for any damaging effects on her kidneys. This chemo combo was also known to affect her high frequency hearing, which she still struggles with even today. The treatments continued every six weeks for a year and a half. She was on Zofran for nausea and lost her hair several times.

Lauren was unable to return to school that year but she did receive her First Holy Communion in April, attending that special Mass in a wheelchair. When she went back to school the next year, she repeated second grade. Lauren's teacher, Mrs. Sego, was once again a godsend, helping take urine samples while Lauren was at school so Bunny could get them to the doctor for analysis. Lauren went to school for an hour or so at a time but not when her white count was low. She missed birthday parties and learned to live without her beloved sports. Even now she has to work harder at her studies since the brain trauma left her with some learning disabilities.

Today, Lauren is considered cured. She still has scheduled MRIs—in the beginning, she went every three months, then every six months and now, she has one every nine months.

Throughout this harrowing experience, both parents say they could never have made it without the loving support system of family and friends. Both sets of grandparents were on call, providing whatever help was needed. They were Ryan's caregivers and his lifeline. Bunny and Kevin give Ryan much-deserved credit for being understanding, supportive, and even learning to become more independent. "Ryan was strong," says Kevin proudly. "He did a lot for himself at the time. We stayed in touch daily with cell phones but I still think it was difficult for him. But he was such a trooper." And so was Lauren. "I don't know if she realizes how sick she was," says Bunny. "Medicine was a part of her life for two years but she never complained. We would see other kids crying and not wanting to be there. Not Lauren. Even now, she works out twice a week to build her muscles. She is still weak on her left side and has balance issues. The doctors say if she can build the muscles, she will overcome it. She worked out yesterday at Cohen's gym. She never complains. She knows she'll have to do this the rest of her life."

Lauren and Ryan are now typical teenagers with their share of healthy arguments and drama. "But deep down, she holds a special place in his heart," says Bunny of the sibling relationship. "He knows what she went through and I think that makes him love her more. He's had to write essays at school and he chose to write about what his sister had to go through. That's how I know he may look all tough on the outside but has a big heart."

There were too many friends involved to ever mention them all, but Bunny especially appreciates a co-worker who graciously took on Bunny's workload that year so Bunny could keep her job. There were church friends who surprised the family with a low country boil to raise money for their expenses. The extended family, on both sides, were the mainstays who helped with Ryan and kept a level of normalcy in his life throughout Lauren's recovery. There were blessings in the form of meals, pet care, house cleaning and prayers. These people helped turn a Friday the 13th tragedy into a miracle.

"I know that things happen for a reason," says Bunny. "There's a reason this happened to Lauren but I feel like she had to go through this to show other people. There were kids we met that didn't make it and they didn't make it for a reason. God only knows why and I don't question it. Before, if she sneezed, it was just a cold. But now, any little thing gets my attention. I don't take anything for granted anymore."

## TWO YEARS LATER

Lauren has been cancer free now for almost ten years. She is a junior at Saint Vincent's Academy. Lauren continues to struggle through school due to the effects of radiation and chemo. But thanks to recommendations from her doctor and Saint Vincent's making accommodations for her, she is doing well. "We are still not sure what her future holds, but we do know that we have to take one day at a time," says her mother, Bunny. "She is happy and loving life. And we are loving her."

# Ajani Brisbane
## One Athletic Amputee

Most moms just shake their heads at how often they have to replace a child's tennis shoes. They grow out of them or they ruin them with their rough play and have to be replaced at least twice a year. For Ragan Flowers, though, it isn't just the shoes her active child wears out, but also his prosthesis.

Ajani Brisbane is one heck of an athlete, a budding musician and a proficient artist. He's all boy with piles of energy and a zest for life like any 10-year-old. He's also an amputee who has never let his artificial limb slow him down.

Ragan learned something was amiss when she was 16 weeks pregnant. The ultrasound technician saw a difference in the length of her baby's legs and detected a hole in his tiny heart. Ragan was prepared for a medical battle and it came early on. Ajani stayed in the hospital two weeks after his mother went home. During that time, he developed an infection in his chest from the hole in his heart. He finally came home and spent an uneventful first year growing and developing. Around his first birthday, he underwent open-heart surgery to close the hole. That's the same time that Ragan started worrying about the difference in the lengths of his legs and began consulting doctors. Before long, it was determined he had right hip dysplasia. Due to the missing tibia in his right leg, his right thigh was shorter and curved outward and required surgery. Ajani was three when doctors operated on his hip and amputated part of his foot. There were other options that Ragan considered, but she chose the solution that involved the least amount of trauma to her son. She didn't want to have the leg lengthening surgery. She was worried other options would require multiple surgeries for the rest of his childhood years.

"They took off the front of his foot," explains Ragan, "from the toes to the middle. Then they moved the heel to the front to give him a pad for walking." After two and a half months in the hospital, Ajani was fitted for his first prosthesis and learned to walk on it a few months later.

"He did awesome," says the proud mom. "You could never tell that he even had [the prosthesis]. He didn't have to go to physical therapy. He didn't have to have anyone show him or teach him how to use it. He put it on and hit the ground running. There was hardly any adjustment period. It was amazing!"

Since that first artificial limb, there have been many to follow. Not because he's had problems with a prosthetic, but because he outgrows it or breaks it. During recent growth spurts, Ragan has had to replace the prosthetic about every six months.

The independent young man doesn't want help and doesn't want to be treated differently from the other kids. During a recent visit to get his (broken again) new prosthesis, he asked the nurse, "Why do you keep asking me if I need help?"

Ajani needs no help with his many activities, either. He's a talented artist, is taking electric guitar lessons and wants to start martial arts. But where he shows his spirit and determination most is on the soccer field. For several years, he has played in a Brunswick league and never let his prosthesis get in the way of protecting the goal. "At the time the other sports teams weren't allowing him to participate," recalls coach Shawn Williams. "His condition was a barrier. His mom asked for my advice and I just told her there was one program available—soccer."

Ajani and his (now) 9-year-old sister, Inaja, both joined up and both were soon proficient athletes. "He's really good," says his proud mom. "His coach says he can eyeball another player as he's dribbling and steal the ball from him in two seconds. He gets it perfect every time. I can't figure out how he does it. He's a very good runner, he's just a little slower."

But as the "keeper" on the field and off, there's nothing slow about Ajani. In fact, he's become an inspiration to his teammates. "He just always gives his best," says Shawn. "He's always providing encouragement to the other kids. Once they found out he had an artificial limb, they wanted to know more about it. They talk about how he's out there and he's giving his all. He's overcoming challenges in his life and not letting limitations prevent him from doing anything he enjoys." Shawn says the other kids have a greater sense of appreciation for their own abilities, thanks to Ajani. "He's just been a joy. He's always laughing, he's upbeat, and he always wants to dance. His enjoyment of life is contagious."

Ajani's spirit comes not only from within but from a mother whose parenting philosophy nurtured his independence. "I am raising him like every other kid," says Ragan. "They (his teachers) have asked me to get a handicapped bus to come get him. I don't want to do that; he doesn't need that. He can do flips and handstands. There's nothing he can't do. I don't want him to think he has any limitation."

It's still up in the air whether or not Ajani will play soccer again this year. He's been there, done that and now wants to pursue a sport that involves *catching* a ball. Ajani knows the sky's the limit and has no doubt whatsoever that he'll do well in any and all endeavors he undertakes.

*Shawn Williams has been asked to start a soccer program for special needs children in the Brunswick area but is concerned there aren't enough volunteers to staff such an ambitious project. His current soccer program encourages father participation, has an academic and literacy component, and even career exploration for older children. His group started out as a way to bring minorities into the sport of soccer and has turned into a life course for parents and kids. If you'd like to know more about programs available, contact the Georgia Youth Soccer Association.*

## TWO YEARS LATER

Ajani is now 12-years-old and is a 7th grade student at Brunswick Christian Academy. This summer he graduated as the valedictorian of his class for the College of Coastal Georgia "Boys of Summer Program" sponsored by the "14 Black Men of Glenn." This program has been in operation for many years and Ajani was even offered a $1000 scholarship for finishing top of his class. He was also the keynote speaker for the summer program's graduation ceremony. Ajani still loves sports and plans to play basketball for BCA this upcoming season.

# Maria Milik

## Together We Win

Maria Milik is a self-professed Type A personality. In her early professional years, she was an associate museum curator—a workaholic dynamo. A later-in-life baby turned her into a workaholic, professional *mother/advocate* who can, and will, move mountains for her two handsome boys.

Maria knew pregnancy wouldn't be easy for her. She had a history of back problems and doctors weren't sure she would be able to carry a child to term. Epidurals were out of the question. Her all-natural delivery produced a beautiful, screaming, healthy, 7-pound boy with a good Apgar score. But her instincts told her something was wrong when baby Leo wouldn't stop screaming. He cried 15-20 hours a day, never sleeping more than 20 minutes at a time.

At eight weeks old, Leo threw up blood and that was it. Maria decided she wasn't taking him back to the pediatrician; instead she went straight to the children's hospital 45 miles away to begin an exhausting and frustrating weekly regimen of trial-and-error treatment. After a battery of tests, doctors determined that there was a feeding problem and suggested a gastric tube. At the same time these drastic measures were being recommended, a friend (who happened to be a nutritionist) suggested a dietary change. Maria decided to give it a try. After trying 17 months worth of traditional treatment, the best doctors in the region, a slew of medications and still no answers, she decided to try her friend's suggestion.

"I tried the diet—no gluten or dairy—and in just three days he was a different child," remembers Maria. "Two weeks later, we saw our case worker who was stunned and wanted to know what we did." Leo had progressed from a child who could not participate in productive play to one stacking blocks and *smiling*! "He stopped throwing up and went from a miserable to happy baby overnight. It was wild!" said Maria. The sickly baby who had already had chicken pox, hand/foot and mouth disease, back-to-back ear infections and severe stomach issues was better! Suddenly, there was no more screaming, he was sleeping through the night and life was significantly better—not perfect, but better.

Unfortunately, the positive effects of the diet and Leo's improving health were not long lived. At about 28 months, he came down with a devastating virus that brought on severe diarrhea for eight to ten weeks. It didn't take long for Maria to realize that his communication skills were declining as well. He had always been behind developmentally but had been improving thanks to early intervention therapy. Then one of his therapists said the words Maria will never forget. She suggested Maria have Leo "evaluated." She thought he might have autism. Maria was stunned. "I thought she'd overstepped the line. 'No way,' I told her. 'This kid's sick. What if you were throwing up every day of your life, had horrible diarrhea and had to go to work and be productive?'" Even the doctors dismissed the idea. But finally, when Leo was about 3, Maria gave in. "Before, I didn't really think he had autism—I thought that was baloney," recalls Maria. "Then, I finally had to realize it was true."

Six years later, one would never know what Leo (and his mother) went through to get him to the full-functioning, happy, healthy child he is today. Looking back, Maria believes the initial bout with diarrhea was caused by the Rotavirus and may have triggered autism symptoms. All she knew for sure was that Leo was severely allergic to gluten products. After reading Dr. Doris Rapp's book, "Is This Your Child?," she found a doctor who would administer provocation neutralization testing (or P-N for short). This series of tests is similar to the allergists' prick tests. A potential allergen is injected in the blood stream. There's a ten-minute wait and if there's a reaction, a smaller dose is injected until the condition is neutralized. The immune system is eventually strengthened over time. The P-N testing and the change in diet was "HUGE!" said the exuberant mom. "Leo was allergic to a plethora of different elements—molds, clover, pollen, chlorine and so many foods. When we had him tested for bananas, the diarrhea hit before he stood up from the chair. We had to change him three times during that testing. Bananas! We'd been feeding him bananas for years!"

Maria's relentless research brought about another major breakthrough; she suggested Methyl B-12 shots. The doctor agreed. Maria began giving them every three days per the doctor's instructions. Six hours after his first shot Leo walked up to Maria, who was filling out yet another doctor's form and said his first sentence ever, "Mom, are you done yet?" Maria started crying. Leo had never said more than two words and had never posed a question before. "This was a major wow," his mother recalls. His expressive language boomed from there. By the time the summer was over, he had *exceeded* his individual education plan (IEP) goals to be completed for the next year. Maria doesn't take all the credit for these many successes. She looked for the right doctor as diligently as she studied potential treatments. She credits the doctor's ability to work with a mother's instincts and his flexibility to form a working partnership on behalf of her child's changing needs.

When Leo was 5 and still on baby food because of a severe gag reflex to solid foods, Maria took her next big leap. She discovered successes in other patients with autism taking Low Dose Naltrexone, which is used with MS patients and other extreme conditions. As the LDN cleared up some of the "fogginess" that produced the gag reaction, Leo was soon eating solids and consuming more food than he had in three years of eating therapy. While on this therapy, potty training was finally completed after five years. This was all a huge relief to the stressed mother who had given her child the Heimlich three times in one week to keep him from choking to death. She was on high alert and was hesitant to leave him with babysitters for fear the worst could happen. But the treatment didn't last long. After seven months, he developed a rash at the site of those shots and they had to stop. But thankfully, he had been on LDN long enough that he didn't lose the benefits and continued progressing, to the joy and relief of Maria.

Throughout all these trials (and yes, there were errors), Leo underwent all types of therapies that were available. He went to occupational therapy, physical therapy, speech therapy—you name it—the Miliks had Leo involved. One very successful program and fun for him was therapeutic horseback riding. His mom became very active in the program and was even called upon to write articles and was interviewed for a promotional video.

As demanding as Leo's progress was on the family, he wasn't the only one needing mom's attention. When Leo was three-and-a-half, Maria and her husband, Jack, welcomed a new baby into their home. Joey was the easy child. "I had Joey, who would wake up every two or three hours and go back to sleep! This was what it is supposed to be like with a new baby! I had no idea [after Leo]." At 28 months (the same age as Leo when he was affected) Joey came down with what Maria believes was the same Rotavirus, and his development stalled. "After six weeks with the virus, he came out of it hand slapping, banging his head on the floor, rocking himself to sleep, toe walking—all signs of autism," remembers Maria. "The first time around we didn't know what it was. We didn't know what signs to look for. We knew nothing about autism. This time we did."

He started wheezing, had ear infections, and showed signs of allergic tendencies. Maria took him off dairy products.

At Maria's insistence, Joey was tested for copper, zinc and lead levels. Three days later, the doctor called Maria to tell her Joey's zinc was dangerously low. "Most kids with autism have low zinc levels. They need zinc to eliminate copper. If the copper is too high, they retain heavy metals and get the serious, cognitive brain problems," said Maria. Today, Joey has an IEP and undergoes occupational and speech therapy for minor issues. Both boys are "extremely smart," says the proud mother, and almost symptom free. "They're still a work in progress, but what kids aren't?"

As Leo and Joey improved, Maria found herself getting involved in the autism community—educating, advocating, fund-raising and sharing her art history background with various projects.

She's currently working with *Express Yourself,* a series of shows and books featuring the works of special needs children that's the brainchild of philanthropist and artist Thomas Balsamo. Her job involves everything from writing press releases to setting up gallery exhibitions, hanging the pieces on the wall and handling the invitations and promotion. The team hopes to expand to a traveling show featuring special artists from all over the country.

The beautiful autism mom worked with Polly Tommey, the creator of "Autism Mother's Campaign," which is a heart-stopping video featuring mothers of kids with autism from all over the country and the world. Maria organized a photo shoot of women in Chicago and is featured in the YouTube video with those moms. You can google the video with the powerful theme, "Together We Win." Maria has also worked closely with Autism One, Special Education Forum, Barrington Early Learning Center, Walk On Farm Therapeutic Riding Center and BASV (Barrington Area Special Voices).

After all she's been through with her children, she says she feels like a Post Traumatic Stress Disorder patient. But she looks at her boys who are both "on timeline" and counts her blessings. "The boys love each other to death. They fight like cats and dogs, which drives me nuts. But they're doing great." says Maria. "What do I tell people? Nothing's fool-proof. Every child is different. You'll never know what triggers the problem. It was hard fought like you wouldn't believe. What we did has worked. We kept trekking along, made steady progress and we're exhausted. But every single bit of it has been worth it."

## TWO YEARS LATER

Leo (a fifth grader) has been progressing nicely in school and at home. He started on NeuroProtek (a Mast Cell Inhibitor) and he has made great gains. His allergies are 80% better. He is able to attend to his schoolwork for a longer period of time; his handwriting has improved and he looks and feels much better. Last year he received an almost perfect score of all As! He still has an aid in the classroom but has become more independent as each year goes by. Joey (now in second grade) is also progressing wonderfully. He also has an aid to help with attention and focus in school. Maria is co-authoring a book that will be finished by the end of the school year. She has started a new organization called AutismFreeBrain and continues to write for The Autism File Magazine as a volunteer. And finally, in addition to all her volunteer work, she has started a new business called Box Organix (www.boxorganix.com).

# A Very Special Prom Queen
## Rosie Wins!

Glenda Williams didn't really want to encourage her 21-year-old daughter Rosie to run for Prom Queen. The special needs student had recently lost a similar bid for homecoming just a few months before. But Glenda soon learned that her unflappable child had a mind of her own and an ace up her sleeve. She was one of the most beloved students at Windsor Forest High School. When she threw her hat into the ring for the title of queen, Rosie won it hands down!

"I was happy," recalls the bubbly Rosie. "You know how you have this feeling something good is going to happen? I had that feeling. I won! I won by a landslide!" It was true. After the traumatic and heartbreaking loss for homecoming queen, Rosie was rewarded by her friends with the crown at prom. Her mother was stunned.

"I never heard of anyone in a high school Special Education class winning prom queen," said her mother. "Never thought it in a million years. Her art teacher, Mr. Blair, told her not to listen to me. He said she should run."

Jeremy Blair is the art teacher who made a much greater impact on Rosie than just encouraging her bid for prom court. He also helped her develop to her full artistic potential.

When Jeremy first met Rosie, there was a tendency among teachers to overlook the Special Ed students. He knew educators who just put the kids down at tables with some crayons and paper and left them to their own devices. But Jeremy saw ability in Rosie and discovered his own challenge. Under his patient tutelage, Rosie became the star of Windsor Forest's art program and began winning local, state and national art competitions. And seldom, in any of the applications for these contests, was Rosie's condition ever mentioned.

Rosie's handicap was evident to those around her but never clearly diagnosed. The doctors discussed her developmental delays with her mother and hinted at some sort of autism. "She is not a severe case," says her mom, Glenda. "She always liked patterns, polka dots, stars and moons." When Rosie first started school, she wouldn't sit with the group and her teacher had to hold Rosie in her lap so she couldn't wander. Rosie had a lot of fears. She struggled with potty training. She didn't eat solid food until 14 months old. She didn't walk until she was about 15 months old. Thanks to a lot of hard work and a love of learning, she is a proud graduate of Windsor High School's Special Education program.

Her first few years at Windsor weren't exactly memorable. But slowly and without much effort, her infectious, loving personality won over her classmates and she became one of the most popular kids in school. The fact that she was undeniably the most prolific artist in the school most certainly helped elevate her status among her peers. She could draw and paint, but she also mastered the computer arts manipulating her digital photography. She was a genius with film and video, editing her own works. And her accomplishments were getting her noticed and bringing home top honors and awards. "She made an animation where she turned on a faucet and blue plastic water blew out of the faucet," recalls Jeremy proudly. "Blue plastic water shot out of her ears. It was incredibly creative."

Rosie's mom first thought her child was winning all these contests because she was being labeled as a Special Education student. But she soon realized that her child was competing against *all* kids on an even playing field—even students in art magnet schools! Since those early days in "Mr. Blair's class," Rosie has become known in the art world, even exhibiting in the "I Have Marks to Make" Exhibition at the Jepson Center last March. There, she *made her mark* as the first student to exhibit a video piece in the show, which is specifically designated for special needs artists.

But if Rosie is making her mark, it isn't just in the art world she has stormed and conquered, it's in the lives of the people blessed to know her. "Rosie taught me about how to treat another person," said Jeremy. "Being an adult, I assumed I knew how to communicate and treat people well. The way she communicates with people and the way she treated me was beyond anything I had ever seen before. I am a Christian person and I've always believed in God my whole life. I'd never had any challenging moments, not like Rosie. But I could see God working through Rosie all the time. The main thing she taught me was no matter what you do in life, you have to treat everyone equally."

Jeremy recalls Rosie's years at Windsor: "[Other students] knew she had a low IQ but once we began to exhibit her artistic talent and she was able to show how talented she is, her confidence began to grow," he says. "Then the other students could see her beauty, how wonderful she is to everyone. People just wanted to be around her. And they wanted to be like her."

So it was no surprise when the 2010 Windsor Forest Prom Queen was announced and it was no surprise when the student body began chanting, "Rosie, Rosie, ROSIE!" The beautiful, shy young girl, considered "slow" by some had raced ahead of the class because of her infectious laugh, her kind heart and her determined spirit. Though she credits her beloved "Mr. Blair" with all of her achievements, he credits *her*. "I concentrated on helping her exhibit her talents and she made herself a star. She [was voted prom queen] because her fellow students genuinely loved her because of the way she treated people. It was her own spirit that came out and people loved her for it."

A side note to this story—Jeremy offered to escort Rosie onto the football field when she ran in the Homecoming Court and lost. She took him up on that offer and was grateful he was there to support her when she didn't win. He told her then and he told her again when it was time for run for Prom Queen, "All things are possible," he said. "You never know if you can win unless you try. If you don't try you might regret later that you didn't try. Better try and lose than not try at all."

Rosie also used her persuasiveness to promote her favorite teacher. She nominated him for WTOC-TV's 2010 Teacher of the Year and he won. She did it all on her own. She called the station, filled out the application and was delighted to see Mr. Blair featured in the news. "I'm grateful for that," says Jeremy. "She hasn't just helped me personally but she also gave me something I could put on my resume!"

Jeremy has taken his own advice ("all things are possible") to heart. He is now studying for a doctorate in art at the University of North Texas. He credits Rosie for his confidence to make this giant step. She played a key role not only in his upgraded resume but also his new philosophy toward teaching. "Thanks to Rosie, I learned to treat every student—whether they were in a wheelchair or a slow learner—as if he or she were equal to me in value and intelligence. After Rosie had modeled these behaviors for me, I changed how I taught my class. Now we teach them to sew or shoot photography or edit video. I made a commitment to do the same things with a special needs class that I would do with a regular class."

So, who's the teacher? Who taught whom?

"I'm excited to be a part of her life," says Jeremy. "I told her she was going to have a way better future than I will. I am fully convinced she has everything figured out. Maybe not in paying bills or the normal adult stuff but in the stuff that matters. Her connections with people and her connections with God are what matters."

Since graduation, Rosie has won two first-place awards at the Coastal Empire State Fair for her artwork and that, says Jeremy, is his and her greatest testimony. "I wanted to train Rosie for the future, so that when I moved on, she could still be creating and submitting her art. Instead of just sitting around and giving up on her abilities, just because I'm not there or because she's not in school, she can keep working. And she has proven herself. I'm thrilled that she is continuing her work and her family is supporting her efforts."

"I'm glad God put me and Mr. Blair together," says Rosie. "I call him on the phone sometimes. We talk."

## TWO YEARS LATER

Rosie's beloved "Mr. Blair" left Savannah in 2010 and began work on his doctorate at the University of North Texas. He is through with his course work and is working on his dissertation here in Savannah. He is currently working as an art educator at the STEM Academy while finishing his work. He has started a new program, which he calls the intersection of art and technology. Rosie attended the open house at Mr. Blair's new school where her cousin attends. He continues to encourage Rosie to pursue her art and independence. They talk every couple weeks about her ideas and her life. Mostly, Rosie loves to re-tell the story of her prom queen election. Mr. Blair reminds her that EVERY SINGLE PERSON in the senior class voted for her. That's something Rosie never bores of hearing and something her former teacher loves to reminisce about as well.

# The Common Thread

### Four Special Families on One Miracle Street

On a normally quiet cul-de-sac here in Savannah, pandemonium can break out at any given time. That is, if the weather's nice and the boatloads of kids who live on this street all happen to be home—ready to bolt from the confines of the house and get out to play. What makes this All-American scenario unique is the similarities in each of the households and how they all ended up on this street at very crucial moments in their lives. They are all military families and have lived through their fathers'/husbands' deployments.

As if those similarities weren't enough to tie their hearts and their lives together, the mothers also forged a bond over their shared faith in God and their devotion to their children, and some are even learning to sew as a group. But the common thread that binds them for life is the children in their lives. Each has a beloved son or daughter with a special need. Here are their stories.

# Genevieve and Alma:
## Surviving a second Brain Surgery

Genevieve and Louis Espinosa have five children between them, three girls who currently live with them. Alma is their special child. When she was younger she seemed to have trouble learning to read. She was tested and declared "gifted" with an IQ of 113. At the time, Genevieve was a single mother, muddling through as all parents do. She believed the doctors that Alma may be dyslexic with ADHD and dealt with those diagnoses accordingly.

Several years later, Alma began having headaches. The family made numerous visits to the doctors at the military bases where they lived. Sometimes she was treated for migraines. Alma was having problems in school and the doctors would change her medicines. Finally, after several months of trial and error, a CT scan was scheduled.

Genevieve suspected something was wrong when she was told she couldn't see the brain scan. Just a few hours before, the nurses had said Genevieve *and* Alma could see the scans. After lunch, Genevieve got a call telling her the CT scan needed further evaluation. They told her to return immediately to the hospital emergency room because the neuro unit was nearby. The now-frantic mother looked at her child and, trying to remain calm, told Alma the doctors needed to take more pictures. Not long after they arrived at the hospital, the family was taken to a waiting room where they learned that Alma had a brain tumor.

"Everything happened so fast," recalls Genevieve. "They gave us the worst possible scenario. IF she survives surgery, she might not survive the chemo. The cancer may have gotten in her whole body."

Alma was rushed into surgery. Genevieve and her daughters were living in Kansas at this time. During the surgery, the doctors came out to tell Genevieve Alma's condition was not what they had suspected. They said it was a cerebellar astrocytoma (a non-malignant tumor). They said they got it all and there was no chance it would return. The tumor was the size of a plum. Alma began physical and occupational therapy. During this whole process, Genevieve and Louis

23

got married, they were transferred to Savannah and, soon after, he was deployed to Afghanistan in January.

While Louis was in the Middle East, Alma went for a routine checkup with her mom. That was when they learned that the tumor doctors said would never grow back, had indeed, grown back. "The good thing about this type of tumor (non-malignant) is that it doesn't spread," says Genevieve. "The bad thing is, it only responds to surgery." After the first tumor was removed, Alma had severe hydrocephalus and Genevieve noticed some personality changes. In spite of the rigid therapy routine, there were changes—especially after the second surgery to remove the returning tumor. There were two years between the two surgeries and it's been a year since the last. "We're about a year out," says Genevieve cautiously. "We're not going to feel better until we pass the two-year mark. Don't know what it's going to do. All we do is watch it."

Two pieces of the tumor were left behind after the second surgery because of danger to the functioning parts of the brain. The doctors aren't sure if these will grow into another tumor. There is always the chance it might return.

Alma turned 15 on May 26 of that year. Her IQ has dropped from 113 to 79 after the two surgeries. With each decision to operate, Genevieve knew there could be damage to Alma's brain—but the alternative wasn't an option. "If we hadn't caught it, she probably would have had a seizure and gone into a coma," says Genevieve. "We took the second tumor out earlier hoping to have less impact on her brain. But we know there is no way you can go into the brain and not have some kind of effect. Nonetheless, we know our child's abilities have changed. The school has tested her and we focus on her positive gifts." Alma is artistic and she has a "sweet soul," says her mom. She participates in an art therapy group and was asked to participate in the "I Have Marks to Make" exhibition at the Jepson Museum. Her pink owls were used as the motif for the invitation to the show.

When Alma underwent her second surgery, the moms on "Miracle Street" had started a Bible study in the neighborhood. They got together once a week. With most of their husbands deployed at the time, mothers got together to pray and study their now-worn Bibles.

Genevieve has a hard time expressing what this group has meant in her life. "We bring each other food and we pray for each others' families. If there's a need with other children, we offer each other a break. When Alma was in the hospital, everybody brought food and came by. I had the opportunity to do that for Melissa when her son was diagnosed with diabetes. We are a shoulder to lean on. Kelly Brown and I do sewing on Thursdays. We all spend a lot of time in doctors' waiting rooms. We don't have much time to socialize and lift each others' spirits, so the time we're together is important. Cindy Keepers' daughter participates in gymnastics with our other daughter. It's an interesting dynamic that so many exceptional families live on this same block."

Before Genevieve knew Alma needed the second brain surgery, the moms were already connected by the Thursday night Bible study at rotating houses. The first topic was called *Living Victoriously During Troubled Times*. Genevieve laughs as she recalls that message, "I love them (the other moms) and think they're wonderful and it has been such a positive experience. I have been part of military life almost my whole life. I know God puts you in a place for a reason and sends you somewhere else for another reason. I know that there are lessons I had to learn here that I'm taking with me somewhere else. This is so unique. I have never had anything like this in all my years in military life. The amount of women involved and the whole neighborhood pulling together is not something you often see."

## TWO YEARS LATER

Alma Espinosa has had a reoccurrence of the tumor but it is small and considered stable. She goes through an MRI every three months to monitor the tumor. She is not symptomatic. Most of it is residual effects of the surgeries. She's cooking, drawing, making jewelry and has decided to be a professional mermaid. She has made "tails" and hopes to rent herself out for pool-side birthday parties. She also plans to live near the ocean when she grows up. Alma has a boyfriend in the Honors program at her high school who plans to go to Air Force Academy. She's enjoying normal teenage activities and she wants to get a job as a bagger at the local grocery store. "The family is currently living in Arizona and plans to retire there," says Genevieve. "But the rest of the time, we keep her focused on being a teenager."

# Melissa and Jacob
## A Type One Diabetes Diagnosis

Twelve-year-old Jacob von Eschenbach was a typical pre-teen. He shot up two or three inches in height from summer to Christmas. He was losing weight, looking taller and lankier, irritable, hungry and thirsty all the time. Just like a typical kid going through puberty. Right? Not exactly.

His mother, Melissa, had no idea that anything was wrong with her active, athletic, handsome son until he woke up the morning he was supposed to take the SAT. He said he didn't feel well, he was insatiably thirsty and he just didn't look like himself. Melissa rescheduled the testing and hoped he would feel better the next day. He didn't. He woke up with a rapid heartbeat, thirsty, his eyes looked sunken and she took him straight to the emergency room.

Melissa had googled his symptoms that morning and was shocked when "Type One Diabetes" popped up. Just a few hours later, the emergency room physician confirmed what she was beginning to discover. Her son was diabetic and spent the day in ICU.

He was soon moved to a regular room in the hospital where he was slowly given insulin. He spent three days in the hospital before he was released to a whole new way of eating and a new approach to his health.

"So many teenagers fit these symptoms and we just attributed it to puberty. He was thin, getting taller, hungry, thirsty, testy. To me that's a normal kid going through puberty," recalls Melissa. "We didn't think anything of it."

It was a shock, to say the least. Jacob was the type of child who seldom got sick. He seldom missed school. He was athletic, loved to be outside and was extremely active. They'll never know if Jacob's diabetes was genetic (Melissa was adopted) or if something in the environment triggered the failure of his pancreas to produce insulin. During the three-day stay in the hospital, the family learned as much as they could. They learned what a good range for blood sugar should be and they learned what to do if it dropped too low. They now know what to do if it gets too high. Jacob learned to give himself a shot with a syringe. He never cried and kept a positive attitude. Melissa was the more emotional of the two, "I cried when the doctor told us."

Jacob could feel the effects of the careful monitoring and it hasn't slowed him down at all. He knows if he follows his medical regimen he'll feel better, have more energy and won't have that thirst sensation nagging at him all the time. He visits the nurse at lunch for accountability, then enjoys his lunch. "I tell him this is a BUMP IN THE ROAD," says Melissa. "I let him know that he hasn't changed much in his life."

Jacob could have gone into a diabetic coma and was actually approaching that dire situation when his parents took him to the ER. His blood sugar was dangerously high. Since then, the von Eschenbachs have changed their diet. They have eliminated sugar drinks—replacing them with diet drinks, Powerade Zero, water. He doesn't even drink orange juice anymore because of the high sugar content. He's cut back on snacks and cakes and has lowered his carbs by about a half his previous intake. Melissa cut out her ritual cookie baking and added cheese and meats to their meals instead of so many breads. Jacob's brothers have learned to "kinda roll with it," says Melissa. "The family's all-around healthier now."

Jacob's been told this will always be a way of life for him. He can be a productive, healthy person—go to college, play sports, lead a normal life—if he can keep his sugar levels and intake maintained and under control.

Melissa and her family weren't this optimistic when they first received the devastating news that Jacob had Type One diabetes. But her "Miracle Street family" gave her and her family members strength when they needed it. "It was the Bible study and my growth toward the Lord over the last year that helped me get through these past couple months. I knew the Lord was standing beside me and would not forsake me or my child," Melissa says. "I think I was put here for a reason. I believe that I was to be a shoulder to cry on for my friends and them for me. We took a year out of our lives and we made beautiful friendships through Bible study. I think we all grew spiritually through that year of support. I call [these women] my sisters. I live on the best street ever."

But these strong women weren't just there for moral support. They provided much needed life necessities during their "sisters'" trials and tribulations. "We would bring meals to each other, watch each others' children. We'd make a phone call, send a text to say 'I'm thinking about you,' meet on the street, whatever it took. Sometimes I'd been thinking, 'I need to cook dinner' but instead, I'm talking to my friends. It was so good for us to talk and have that fellowship and support," said Melissa.

# TWO YEARS LATER

Melissa von Eschenbach shares this update: "It is hard to believe that my active, athletic 12-year-old weighed a mere 87 pounds the day he was diagnosed with Type 1 Diabetes. Today, Jacob is 15, stands just under 6 feet and weighs 178 pounds. He remains extremely active with sports of all kinds. He mostly concentrates on football these days but he also enjoys basketball, track, and rugby. Being a military brat means moving is inevitable. Jacob has had to learn the ropes at two new schools since leaving Savannah. I have learned that each state and school district has different policies concerning diabetic students. Parents, pediatric endocrinologist, diabetes nurse educators and school nurses must come together to make the school environment a positive experience for Type 1 diabetic students. Cindy Keepers and I have remained close since we were fortunate enough to have the Army assign both of our husbands to the Pentagon after Savannah. Living in the same area allowed us to visit and especially watch each other's kids grow and thrive." Jacob's quote about his experience from diagnosis until now: "At first, I thought I wasn't going to be able to play sports but now I'm more active than ever. I think diabetes has helped me become more aware of my health and has been a big learning experience for me." Melissa says, "Jacob's pediatric endocrinologist has been very impressed with his management of his own daily medical care. He has handled this challenge remarkably and has never complained. That is just his personality. He knows he has to control his blood sugar level 24/7 by pricking his finger, testing his blood and deciding how much insulin to inject himself with. He just does it. As his mom, I am so proud of how he has faced this disease 'head on' and has not allowed it to dictate his life."

# Cindy and Erin Keepers

### Battling Multiple Heart Defects in One Child

Cindy and Kirk Keepers knew they were in for the battle of their lives when they learned 26 weeks into their first pregnancy that their unborn child had a severely malformed heart.

But the beautiful, bubbly gymnast who is one of the older children in the Miracle Street playgroup has defied the odds, thanks to the care and determination of her loving parents and excellent doctors.

While still in the womb, the doctors were doling out options. She could have a heart transplant (but they were quick to warn her parents that many babies die waiting for that transplant to become available). Another option was to abort ("*not* an option," said Cindy), and finally, a three-stage protocol called the Norwood Procedure. This is the one they chose and the one they began to prepare for.

Erin was diagnosed with a condition called hypoplastic left heart syndrome. It's one of the most severe of all heart defects or as Cindy describes it, "a lot of heart defects all in one." She was born with half a heart. There was no left side—the most important side that pumps all the blood to the rest of the body. Twenty years ago, hospitals would send afflicted babies home with their parents and tell them to let them die because there was no known treatment. Today, the Norwood Procedure offers a solution that gives families time and, more often than not, a successful outcome.

Cindy moved home to her parents' home in Philadelphia, just 30 minutes from Dupont Hospital in Delaware where Dr. Norwood (who developed the procedure) practices. She stayed there until Erin was born. That's when her newborn underwent her first surgery at just two days old to fix her twisted, underdeveloped heart. She wasn't supposed to have her next procedure for six months but there were complications. Her three surgeries turned into five—all before her first birthday. The final surgery, which is the most crucial, involved rerouting Erin's circulatory system. Her blood flows opposite of ours, her mother explains. It goes straight to her body and then her lungs. "It's amazing," says the proud Cindy. "To look at her you'd have no idea. She doesn't look any different. She's just an average kid."

Erin hasn't had any other major surgeries since then and no other major health issues. But she is carefully monitored. She was a cheerleader at Calvary Day School for fifth-and sixth grade football last year. She takes tumbling classes, is working on her cartwheel and hopes to have her back handsprings perfected before the next football season.

When Cindy moved back to the Savannah area and onto this Miracle Street, one person she met early on was Genevieve because Alma and Erin were already fast friends. The girls bonded easily, talking about their respective surgeries and health histories, but also because they're typical tweens who share that crazy time of learning to grow up. When Kelli (another mom you will read about in the next chapter) arrived in the neighborhood, Cindy was pleased to renew a friendship the two had started years before while Cindy was pregnant with Erin. Throughout the close-knit network of the military, Cindy had kept up with Kelli and knew about Jack's condition (you'll meet Jack in the next chapter) and they were thrilled to be together again and sharing each other's lives.

When Melissa's son, Jacob, was diagnosed with diabetes, Cindy's life came full circle and she was the one giving support. And for Cindy, like the others, she felt the Bible study brought them all together. "I think it's incredible that God put us all together to support each other," says Cindy. "He always finds a way to get people together who need each other. Many of our husbands had been gone for a year. Mine has to come and go. Unfortunately, he's gone more than he's here. We had been through so much with Erin. I always tried to have a positive attitude, but I know it was power from Jesus that put us together in the same neighborhood at this particular time."

While the moms were bonding over Bible study, the kids were sharing and becoming lifelong friends as well. "There were a lot of times where the girls would talk about Erin's heart defect and Alma's brain tumor and what they've been through. The Bible study helped them understand that everything Jesus does is for a reason. And the other kids who were not special needs children really looked at them as role models for their strength and I think the girls put things in perspective for the other kids in the neighborhood," says Cindy. "When the well kids complain about things, they look at Erin and Alma who always have a smile on their faces and have to face so many obstacles. It's an eye opener for the kids who don't have as much to deal with."

Cindy never takes Erin's health for granted. "I think, as a mother of a child with special needs, just to know there's a whole world of moms out there who have these same worries on their mind every day gives me strength," says Cindy. "I feel fortunate that all Erin has is a heart defect. There are so many things that can go wrong, but thankfully, she is doing great. Yes, I worry every day. She probably will need a heart transplant somewhere down the line. I don't know when that will be. We were told maybe at about 10 or 11. But we just saw the cardiologist and he says things look great."

## TWO YEARS LATER

Erin Keepers is fourteen and in the eighth grade and is now living in Madison, Alabama. She started competitive dance two years ago and is on the middle school dance team. When she's not dancing, she's a typical kid—watching TV or eating. She goes back for regular checkups with her cardiologist every six months and continues to receive a clean bill of health. Erin still keeps up with Jacob Eschenbach and sometimes even gets together with their family. Her mom says she is so proud of her for her dancing and her grades (straight As). Cindy reports Thursday's checkup went beautifully and offered to push the visits back to a year. She is on a self-limited status. Her coaches know if she needs to take a break, she can. But Cindy says she's stubborn and rarely takes advantage of that privilege.

# Kelli Brown

## Her Jack Who Lights Up the Room

Kelli Brown's contributions to the afternoon play dates are Jack (now 7 ½) and Jillian who turned 3 in April. Jack is a very special little boy.

After a "blissfully ignorant pregnancy" as Kelli puts it, Jack was born with a cleft palate. That red flag brought on a barrage of doctors and subspecialists. That first midline birth defect triggered testing on his heart, stomach, GI, kidneys and brain. The neurologists began labeling the many conditions that plagued the tiny body. The first geneticist told the new parents Jack wouldn't live six months—that he would die in his sleep.

Jack's immediate concerns were episodes of apnea where his oxygen stats would dip dangerously. When he was finally discharged, he was sent home with supplemental oxygen. He suffered a slew of respiratory related illnesses. The nurses were prophets of doom and gloom.

"We wouldn't take him anywhere, he was a bubble boy," recalls Kelli. "We were so afraid. There's a whole parent psychology you have to come to terms with. You try to accept that you are fortunate to have this child as long as God wants you to keep him. When God wants to call him back, you have to be respectful of that. We live to be thankful of the time we have him." Jack had trouble gaining weight and was soon on a G-tube.

Jack's official diagnosis is chromosomal abnormality. Rather than two of each gene, he has three of the seventh chromosome, which forms a trisomy. And he has only one of the parts of his third chromosome, which is a monosomy. "We have had quite the parent learning curve. It's really interesting that when we've moved and been introduced to a whole new set of doctors and nurses, *we* give the brief," says Kelli. "They look at us and ask if we have a medical background. I just say that I've had five years of residency with Jack. The only things I know about the medical field are things that affect my son. I have the capacity to learn for him."

Kelli's mom lived with her for Jack's first year until the family could get nursing approved. Jack is a 24-hour a day job. Every minute and every hour he required care in the beginning and Kelli said she learned to focus on the most basic needs—breathing and eating. Things went fairly smoothly (as smoothly as things can go under these circumstances). Kelli fought the recommendation to put Jack on a trache, until she finally had to give in. God's hand in the whole process was evident from the beginning.

Kelli and her husband, Jimmy, were out for the evening at the Marine Corps Birthday Ball. The couple that was supposed to join them at their table had fallen ill and two strangers took their place. Jack was home with the nurse and Kelli and Jimmy had brought pictures of their beautiful son to the party. Ever proud of her precious son, Kelli showed the pictures to the newcomers at their table. The wife instantly recognized Jack's condition and she and Kelly began talking about Jack's special needs. This new friend was Dr. Heidi Herrera, who just happened to be a new doctor studying at the Children's Hospital in Washington, D.C. Kelli didn't want to burden the kind physician on her night off, but the two hit it off and shared stories about caring for children with chromosomal abnormalities. "Fast forward a few days later, Jack is unable to breathe. We can't handle him. He was at PICU at Walter Reed, they were trying to intubate him, calling in the anesthesiologists. It was terrifying," recalls Kelli. The doctors at Walter Reed decided he needed to be transferred to Children's Hospital. But there was no room for Jack in the children's NICU.

That's when God and fate stepped in. The physician's assistant at Walter Reed who was relaying Jack's condition to the doctor is saying on the phone, "I have this Jonathon Matthew Brown, father is James Brown. The child has a trisomy . . . is on supplemental oxygen . . . he's been intubated . . . ." Kelli retells the conversation. "All of a sudden, the doctor on the other line told the PA that this condition sounds familiar and she asked if the family calls the child Jack? The PA said 'YES!' Then that person on the other line asked if they call the dad Jimmy and again, the PA said 'YES!'" The hospital had previously told Kelli and Jimmy that there was no room, but then they realized the person on the phone was Heidi! "The light bulb goes on! And this woman, who wasn't even supposed to sit with us at the ball, was telling my husband that she's sending a helicopter to Walter Reed to get Jack!" He was quickly transported, put on a ventilator and the question of whether or not Jack needed a trache was decided for them. He spent three weeks under Heidi's care before he could come home.

Two weeks before, the family had been attending a very progressive, contemporary church service where the minister had asked the congregation to get together and share prayer needs. Jimmy said he wanted Jack to breathe on his own. Two weeks later, the family was given His answer. "I've learned that when God answers your prayers, it may not be the answer you thought you were going to get," says Kelli. "It doesn't mean it's not God's plan. It became clear to us that Jack was just going to have to live with the trache and that he would be better off than before—even though we'd been resisting putting him on it. The ventilator at night helps him stay well because it gives him some reserve oxygen. He isn't always fighting for his breath. Again, it wasn't necessarily what we wanted but it was what God wanted for us."

That's how Kelli and Jimmy look at the move to Savannah. They were stunned to learn that almost every family in their cul-de-sac had a special needs child. "It's remarkable how sharing our stories has given us so much hope and inspiration and has bonded us closer than neighbors regularly would," Kelli said.

Jack attends Juliette Low Elementary School three half-days a week and a nurse goes with him. He is thriving there. He recognizes circles, squares, triangles and rectangles. He's learning to communicate with the many adaptive devices. He rolls over but is still working on sitting up. He participates in physical, occupational and speech therapy and has made great strides. "When Jack smiles, he lights up the room. He kicks his feet when he's happy and he will do the brown frown if he's not happy or if something's hurting him," says his proud mom. "He does express his emotions but 99% of the time he is happy! Take him outside when the breeze blows in the air and he smiles. When he sees a new face, he's happy. He can get loud and rowdy, especially when he's in a church service."

And Jack is usually the center of attention on those many sunny afternoons when the moms and kids of the street gather for play and social time. When Kelli moved to Savannah, the Thursday night Bible study was already underway. With brand new baby Jillian, Kelli wasn't able to get out much. But a new baby fit right in to the loving commotion of the Bible study. And another special needs child certainly didn't shake the mega-moms.

"At first my husband didn't want to accept help," remembers Kelli. "I had to remind him how we feel when we're able to help someone else. I feel that whenever you can help someone, you should do it. And it is also important to accept the fact that you can't do everything. You can't be the perfect family—the super family. You have to grieve the loss of that perfect child, then you look around and realize what you have." Kelli's favorite poem is *Welcome to Holland.* She says it's about someone planning a trip to Italy but when they get off the plane, they're actually in Holland. The premise of the poem is that Holland is a lovely place to be—even if it's not where you thought you'd be.

"There are days when I am just exhausted," admits Kelli. Caring for a special needs child and a newborn will tax any human being. And she's learned to let her friends pick up a grocery item, or bring over a meal or just offer moral support. Her "me" time is spent teaching the other ladies to sew. She monograms the letter O with a hole in the center for Jack's feeding tube to fit neatly into his outfits. She knits her children sweaters during extended stays at the hospital and now she's sharing that talent with her Miracle Street family. "It's how God made us," she says. "We're designed to give and receive and when we let it work that way we're more abundantly blessed. The cohesion it creates is unbelievable. That's what's happened on our street."

*To read "Welcome to Holland" by Emily Perl Kingsley, just google it. The rights are reserved.*

# TWO YEARS LATER

Jack continues to brighten the world with his smiles and happy disposition. He is still fed through his G-tube, on ventilator at night and uses a Smart Vest which helps keep his respiratory system clear and functioning. He has only been in the hospital once (over Thanksgiving last year) and enjoys school and horseback riding. Baby sister, Jillian, is 3-and-a-half and loves to "doctor" her big brother. Her knowledge of medical equipment could well surpass many adults' abilities. Even though the Browns are the last of the original Miracle Street families, God apparently hand-picked new, wonderful neighbors to fill the gap. Kelli's next-door neighbor is a nurse and interior decorator (both much-needed areas of expertise) and another family has adopted the Browns to brighten their holidays. "There's no other way these people could have been put in our lives other than by God answering our prayers," says Kelli. "When it comes about in funny ways, you realize He takes such good care of you."

*As military life goes, so will some of the "sisters" and their families. The von Eschenbachs were transferred to Virginia, as were the Keepers. The Espinosas moved to Arizona. Kelli and her family remain in Savannah for the time being. "It was a sad time. But all of us are so used to moving around that I think we have the faith that things will be okay," says Cindy. "Once again, God will give us the strength and we'll meet other people who will become part of our support group in the future." Cindy's happy about the move, which put her husband working at the Pentagon and home more with the family.*

*So, even though the human landscape has changed on their street, their bonds are forever forged. With the military, families never know when they'll end up together again. "Even if we don't stay in touch, which we most probably will, I'm sure I'll see them again and it'll be as if I saw them yesterday," says Melissa. "Nobody holds grudges (if you don't send a Christmas card) because you'll probably see them again the next Christmas when you get transferred near each other again. Kelli will be the only one left on the block for a while, but a new group of women soon will be here. We (the families who moved) were able to take what we've had here with us and then come back to visit or end up at another post together later on. In fact, I'm pretty confident we'll be together again. In fact, I'm sure we will."*

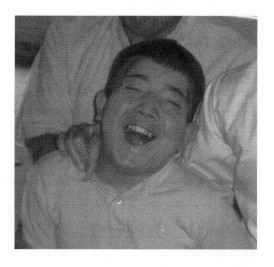

# Will Hall's Story

### "The Faith to Believe, the Hope to Dream and the Love to See it Through." The Joubert Syndrome and Related Disorders Foundation

Era Hall was 35 years old and overjoyed to *finally* be pregnant with her first child. After years of treatment for endometriosis, her dreams of becoming a mother were about to come true. Her husband, Wayne, was just as ecstatic at the news. They, like all new parents-to-be, began preparing for their new addition. Seven months into the pregnancy however, a Level 2 ultrasound indicated an underdeveloped portion of the fourth ventricle of the brain. The doctors were very candid with her; Era learned then that her baby wouldn't have much chance of survival. "I asked God to just give me a baby to take care of. I wanted my own baby that looks like my husband and I wanted him to act like a Opie Taylor," Era says." When they told me about him, I wasn't going to give him back."

"At first they thought it was Dandy Walker Sydrome (a congenital brain malformation involving the cerebellum)," recalls Era. The specialists recommended an amniocentesis, which showed a perfectly normal chromosome count. But still, there was little doubt that something was wrong with the soon-to-be-born baby.

When the beautiful Will Hall entered the world on April 9, 1995, the symptoms of his disorder manifested immediately. Because he had an underdeveloped vermis of the cerebellum, he experienced frighteningly accelerated breathing. At the time, they were still under the assumption that his condition was Dandy Walker Syndrome. But a resident pediatrician at Memorial Health University who had recently read about Joubert Syndrome thought about Will and approached Era with this possibility.

Joubert Syndrome (JS) is a condition that, like Dandy Walker, affects the cerebellum. It's a recessive trait and very rare. A mother in Maryland with two JS children started a foundation for other families of children with this rare disorder. Era learned that a Dr. Flannery from Medical College of Georgia does genetic studies on children with similar symptoms. Dr. Flannery came to Savannah and, after conducting a series of tests, confirmed that Will did have JS. He is one of only two children in this region diagnosed with JS.

After six weeks in Memorial's neonatal unit, Era decided it was time to bring her precious child home. As excellent as the staff was to Will, it was hard to leave her baby every night and not be allowed to return until 7 the next morning. "I had waited for him my whole life and I wanted him home," said Era.

JS affects muscle tone and coordination. As a newborn, Will wasn't sucking and swallowing, and he didn't open his eyes. Even as unresponsive as he was, the staff could tell that Will liked to be held and cuddled under the chin. When Era approached the doctors about taking Will home, she was told that he couldn't survive since he couldn't suck on his own. Era says she put her hands on her hips and defied the doctor, "He does too suck. He did it last night." At the time, a gastric feeding tube was keeping Will alive. It went down the nose, into the back of his throat and into his stomach. Era carefully watched the nurses replace the tube when needed and decided she could do it too. "I told Dr. Smith if eating was the only thing keeping Will from coming home, maybe she could teach me," remembers Era. "And she said, 'you know I think you *can* learn to do that.'"

Era learned how to manipulate the feeding tube, and how to feed Will by holding his chin, cheek muscles, upper and lower lips and bottle all in one hand. With the other hand she had to support his little body. It wasn't easy but she learned to do it. She would do anything to bring her darling baby home.

Her determination paid off. After both Era and Wayne received training on the gastric tube, the apnea monitor and the oxygen machine, the proud parents brought Will home.

Not that it was easy. There was concern that Will had reflux and fear of him aspirating. A simple virus a few weeks after coming home caused him to stop breathing and Era had to give him CPR. He had turned blue. After several of these terrifying episodes, Dr. Cossio recommended the Halls take Will to the Scottish Rite Hospital. They did and stayed there from July until September.

Era can't say enough about the staff and the excellent, extensive care they received at the Scottish Rite. They did a complete workup on every system in Will's body. Era studied and investigated different therapeutic options for Will. They came back to Savannah.

With the help of in-home nurses, Era was able to return to work. Will's gastric tube was replaced to provide him the nourishment he needed to strengthen his disadvantaged little body. His legs could wiggle, but he couldn't use his arms or legs. They found out he was legally blind. He couldn't sit up, hold or reach for things. He couldn't even hold up his head or keep his eyelids open. Every extremity in his body was affected by Joubert Syndrome. There hadn't been much research on this condition at the time and the doctors didn't give him much hope of living more than a year. They didn't know Era and Wayne Hall.

It took a while but the irrepressible Halls finally started seeing improvement. Will participated in therapy programs through Babies Can't Wait and the Savannah Center for the Blind. He underwent speech, occupational and physical therapy. He still had frightening spells where he'd stop breathing. He would get choked on draining mucus and his throat would close up and he couldn't get air. Era had to learn a modified CPR protocol, which she says she repeated at least "a thousand times." At two years old, he was finally old enough for a special cranial facial surgery in Atlanta which stopped the "blue spells." It opened up the airways and made his breathing easier and more consistent.

He did well for another year or so but then blood work came back with a low red blood cell count. At a Joubert Syndrome Foundation function in 1996, Era learned that JS children suffer from kidney malfunction. Will had shown classic symptoms of JS and apparently the kidney issue was no exception. By the time Will was four, another child in the foundation network had developed Stage 4 renal failure and his mother had written an article about his experience. A kidney specialist in Atlanta confirmed that Will's kidneys were failing and told Era he probably wouldn't make the donor list because of his other disabilities. "I was devastated," said Era. "All I could think of was how they were treating prisoners in jail for kidney disease. Surely someone can give one to my child. He was teaching so many people. There were so many good things about my baby."

Will was sent to Egleston Hospital in Atlanta to find out if they would consider treating Will. "I got all my stuff together. I had pictures of Will with family, Will at church. He isn't just a blob sitting there. He made people happy. When people looked at him, he made them smile." Era wasn't going to take no for an answer.

Dr. Hymes and Dr. Warshaw at Egleston agreed with the Halls and began a year and a half of treatments—regulating his feedings, monitoring his bloodwork, and prescribing hormone replacements to increase red blood cell production. Era had to give Will the hormone shot every two days. It wasn't easy, but it kept the kidneys in check.

Will was about to start first grade at May Howard. He weighed a whopping 48 pounds but something was wrong. His stomach and legs were swollen and he was rushed to the hospital. The kidneys were getting worse. He was put on home peritoneal dialysis. He would go to school and come home to do his dialysis. The nurses weren't allowed, under hospital protocol, to do the procedure. Era and Wayne learned to do it. There was a high risk of infection with this kind of home treatment but they did their best to keep the environment as sterile and safe as possible.

Less than a month had passed when they got the call in September 2001 that there was a kidney. Era and Wayne rushed Will to Atlanta where his blood work was miraculously perfect and he was granted the life-saving kidney. The transplant went well, there were no more problems with his kidney and they were able to put dialysis behind them.

Will started getting stronger. Era had been told he was blind, he'd never sit on his own, walk or talk. "I just told them he was precious. It didn't matter." By the time he was 11, thanks to the doctors and orthotics from the Shriners Hospital in Tampa, he could sit up on his own and his legs and arms became stronger. He learned to kick. He learned to kick so hard that last year he kicked a bed railing, trying to get attention, and broke his leg. He had broken his tibia and fibula above the ankle. He was in the hospital from December 19th through the 24th. "That was not what they meant by Christmas break," laughs Era.

There were no other major hospital stays. The specialists would give the Halls direction and they would follow up with Dr. Cossio. Will had good clean kidney function, was developing, getting taller and doing more. He still couldn't walk and talk but he'd learned to communicate in a different way. He was animated, talked with his eyebrows, smiled, laughed and could understand. He started May Howard when he was six and stayed through the sixth grade. In middle school, he went to Myers where the family found Demetra Williams and her para-professionals, Sally Fair and Jessie Brown. "Will loved them to pieces," says Era. And they loved him. "He was nothing but a joy. Will was a very delightful student to have. Even though Will was non-verbal, his receptive skills were high," says Demetra. "You could talk to him. He would respond to us by making little sounds. I might say, 'Are you having a good day?' And he'd say 'ah ahhhh'. . . Some days he would be so noisy and have to get fussed at like a regular kid."

The beautiful boy in the wheelchair became the "man about campus" at Myers Middle School. Everyone knew him and his joy was infectious. He made the teachers and students smile just at the sight of him.

He was a busy young man in and out of the classroom. Era and Wayne took him to the pool where he would float with a balloon pillowing his head above the water and he was able to float on his own. His mother also introduced him to horseback riding. "When we first met the horses, one leaned in and rubbed Will's nose. It touched Will like a marshmellow," recalls Era. "I thought the horse was going to eat Will. But Will laughed so hard. When he giggled his shoulder would shake and of course I had to giggle when Will giggled." And like every other 14-year-old boy, he loved the arcade room, Tilt, at the mall.

He'd come a long way from the baby who'd been given so little hope. "I think he was a miracle. It came from the excellent care of his parents," says his teacher, Demetra. "Once we were in a meeting and the therapist recommended Will stop speech therapy because he had advanced as much as he could. Will's dad turned around and said, 'You can't do this. Why would you take something from him that we feel he truly needs? I don't want any program taken from Will.'" Wayne later told Demetra no matter how little it was, he deserved everything he could get. "Will lacked for nothing," said Demetra, "Care, education, stimulation. Wayne and Era made sure Will had everything he needed while they had him."

And that tenacity paid off with the *gift of a lifetime*. After 14 years, Will finally spoke the words that are music to any mother's ears. Demetra and Jessie caught on tape Will saying to his mom, "I love you."

Will left this Earth on March 7. His parents will never know for sure what brought on the high fever. The doctors think there may have been complications with one of his organs. Whatever the cause, his organs shut down within 24 hours and he was gone. In the few months since Will's death, Wayne and Era have had to learn to live in their house without him. The outpouring of support from those who knew Will has been astounding. Even the children from Will's special needs classroom feel the void. Demetra says there's not a day that goes by without one or more asking her, "Where's Will Hall?"

"All of us need opportunities to do something more and unselfish in our lives," says Era. "It makes us better. There are many opportunities to do for others no matter where you live. I realized how hard Will worked just to be," says Era. "Healthy young people don't understand that they don't have to work to be. They don't take advantage of their advantaged lives. You get a better understanding of your own gifts when you realize how little Will had but what a big gift his whole life was. What a gift to make others laugh, smile, be more caring, maybe think more deeply about their own families or friends or others who were different from them. When he was firstborn, we were so happy to have him, I didn't care what it cost me, I just wanted to keep him."

"He had the cutest little feet," Demetra recalls, "And he'd wear the cutest little sneakers. Those were his trademark-sneakers and sunglasses and precious little hats. Will was a well-taken-of child. He was a well-loved child. I can't praise his parents enough for taking such good care of Will. He left us knowing he was a well-loved child."

"He was teaching me and others. He was teaching my husband," Era says proudly. "Wayne did things like give Will CPR, he was the first to give Will a shot, set up oxygen," says Era. "Wayne did things I never thought he could do. I saw a gift in my husband I didn't know he had. I think any child brings that out. But Will especially did.

"Sometimes, I almost wander around and I feel useless. Even though I have my students at school, Will gave my life such purpose. We knew what we were doing when we had to feed him, get him to therapy, give him his meds. We don't have nurses in our home anymore. No schedule. I feel purposeless. I know how to take care of a child and there's no one to take care of. I don't feel cheated. I feel like I'm having to wait for whatever venture my life still has to take and I don't have any road plans yet.

"My faith taught me that the sun rises and the sun sets and genetic information changes hands. If all the genetic information is not there, it's going to do what laws of nature says will happen. I believe God steps in when we have faith to believe there is going to be another day. My attitude is we're going to live with joy because Will's life was joy; just because he couldn't sit up and swallow too well doesn't mean there wasn't joy in that life. I found the good and the beauty in Will and the good things he could do. In all things, God works together for the good. I found the good. I found good in people—good doctors, good therapists, the Shriners, the equipment that supported his little body so well. They were all awesome. We found all the good we could and the good came back to us."

Whenever Era's asked how she manages to smile throughout all the difficulties and even after the death of her only child (she was and is asked this often), she responds simply: "We had to choose our attitude. We chose to be joyful because Will was with us. We made that decision. We were not going to cry, not going to feel sorry for ourselves, but be joyful that we had him with us and we are."

This is the hymn that was sung at Will's funeral. It's called *The Hymn of Promise.*

In the bulb there is a flower; in the seed, an apple tree;
In cocoons, a hiding promise: butterflies will soon be free!
In the cold and snow of winter there's a spring that waits to be,
Unrevealed until its season, something God alone can see.

There's a dawn in every darkness, bringing hope to you and me.
From the past will come the future; what it holds, a mystery,
Unrevealed until its season, something God alone can see.

In our end is our beginning; in our time, infinity;
In our doubt there is believing; in our life, eternity,
In our death, a resurrection; at the last, a victory,
Unrevealed until its season, something God alone can see.

Era Hall served on the board of the Joubert Syndrome and Related Disorders Foundation for ten years. During that time, she and her fellow board members broadened awareness of the condition by starting e-mail conversations, creating a website in 1998, formed a Yahoo group and established a network of specialists, doctors and families throughout the world. She has attended JS Foundation Conferences, the Pediatric Neurology Conference in Washington, D.C., and is currently JS Foundation regional coordinator. Her dream is for JS to become like chicken pox or small pox—treatable and eradicated. She was inspired by a speaker's opening line, "let our ceiling be someone else's floor." In the meantime, the foundation works for more research, networking and awareness. Its motto is, "The faith to believe, the hope to dream and the love to see it through."

## TWO YEARS LATER

Era Hall says the last three years have seen many tears but she and her husband hold on to their faith that Will's work was done. She believes God needed another cymbal player on his knee, another giggling boy for His choir. Since her son's passing, she has stayed busy, trying to fill the empty place left in her heart. Era has written her own story about Will that she shared with family and friends. She continues to work in the school system and has recently accepted a position in the Exceptional Child Program for 3rd Grade Inclusion. She remains active in community organizations and has attended two Joubert Syndrome and Related Cerebellum Disorder Foundation Conferences. Era's incredible outlook on life (in spite of the loss of her precious Will) is explained in this comment: "If I could hang on to Will's coattail when it's my time, I know he would fly me straight to his new home in Heaven," writes Era. "He was an amazing boy—full of love for everyone when given the chance. His smile always brightened my world."

# Julie Coy and her "Cool" Son, Grant
## 'Art'ism Advocate

Her son is a making a name for himself in the international art world. He has won numerous awards, is featured in galleries and traveling shows and he has earned over $6,000 for one piece. Julie Coy and her son, Grant Manier (pronounced maun-yay), have come a long way.

Twelve years ago, Julie was a single mom raising her sons, 4-year Ross and 8-year-old Grant. To make ends meet, Julie got a job at a special school for children with autism in Houston, Texas. At the time, this working mom thought autism manifested itself in severe behavior. Her first week at Westview School, working with these special children, was a shock. She realized these children were just like her Grant. "Eleven years ago, autism wasn't prevalent. I had heard and seen head banging and several people would tell me something was not right with Grant," Julie recalls. "He looked so normal with perfect physical abilities. His speech was echolalic (immediate and involuntary repetition of words or phrases) and he could recite "Thomas the Tank Engine" lines all day but couldn't really dialogue with others. He also had some obsessions."

Recognizing the similarities between Grant and her students, Julie had to admit to herself that Grant was a child with autism but very high functioning. "It blew my mind. I recognized it when I saw all those kids. My heart just dropped. We knew we were having problems—thunder, socialization, anxiety. More and more, I knew it was autism. The signs were all there. Once, when Grant was attending public school, I overheard a little girl say, 'get away, you weirdo,' and that was in first grade." That's when Julie and her director at Westview found a place for Grant at their school.

Grant was first diagnosed with pervasive development disorder (PDD), which encompasses a wide range of neurological conditions. Julie knew there was more and eventually got the autism diagnosis. Early intervention was now the key. For three years Grant continued at Westview, developing social skills through public interaction. Later, in a public school fifth grade class, Julie decided it was time to try home schooling. Her son "with the heart of a gentle bear" was subjected to bullying. As frustrating as it was to see kids being unkind to her child, it turned out to be a turning point in Grant's life.

Working one-on-one with her precious son, Julie and others always knew Grant had artistic talent. He was excelling in his academics but had time on his hands. To complement his curriculum, Julie decided to revive an old habit of Grant's. When he was small, he loved to tear paper. Any paper. He'd shred it into tiny pieces and leave it in piles on the floor. The first time she suggested he use paper again as an artistic tool, he was about to paint a sun. Instead of painting a yellow ball, he created a magnificent collage of yellows, greens and purples using over 3,500 pieces of shredded recycled paper. "My friend saw it and was like, 'That is *amazing!*' And so did the art consultant who saw it and agreed!" said Julie. The sun piece was so successful, Grant began making more as part of his academic curriculum or some other activity he enjoyed. When he was working on social studies, he created a piece on Mount Rushmore and another of the American flag with a bald eagle in the foreground. He has always enjoyed therapeutic horseback riding so he did a beautiful work on his favorite Appaloosa. The 16-year-old young man expanded his materials to include the top layer of puzzles and made a butterfly representing his impression of the autism symbol. The beauty of his work, the skill of his artistry and the uniqueness of his finished pieces have made him famous in the art world.

Grant has already sold one piece for $6,400. Last year, he took top honors in the Austin Rodeo Eco Art Grand Champion exhibition. He's been featured in magazines, local newspapers and on television stations. He was the featured artist at the Autism Speaks Walk in Houston, his work and was featured in the Dallas Museum of Art, and he will exhibit at many other art events in the coming year. Grant designed the flyer for the "Give Autism A Chance" campaign. Grant is going to be featured in a book *The Art of Autism: Shifting Perception,* which showcases artists with autism. His inaugural calendar, the 2012 Eco-Impressionist Calendar—featuring 12 of his colorful, creative pieces successfully sold out. Grant was awarded the 2011 Houston Mayor's Disabilities Youth Advocate of the Year. All this new-found attention doesn't go to the young celebrity's head. "He takes it so casually, bless his heart," laughs his mom.

Grant calls his collages "COOLages." What's so "cool" about Grant is not just his incredible talent, but also his innate desire to help others. Grant donates his work and proceeds from his work to local fund-raisers and non-profits. At the Autumn's Dawn Gala, Grant's works sold for $7,500 and he donated a percentage of the proceeds back to the organization. His choice of materials isn't just coincidence. He's also aware of our delicate environment so his choice of materials is always well planned. He teaches children how to COOLage while being environmentally responsible by "reducing, reusing and recycling" materials.

Grant says his autism is an art. In his bio he says, "I'm a voice for those you cannot hear and I lead by example for those you cannot understand." His passion for his peers is never more evident than when he is advocating for job opportunities. "He understands how his friends are struggling to get and keep jobs." Grant is in the process of acquiring a copyright on a logo he's designing to promote autism employment. When he was just nine, Grant co-wrote his first book, *Dear Journal, I Have Autism.* This heartfelt account of his struggles gives others hope. "I'm really hoping my work teaches other people they can do things. I'm trying to help them find their genius and hope their parents can realize their potential like my mom did."

Grant's brother, Ross (now 20), is also a gifted artist but says his brother has more patience. "He's proud of me," says Grant. "And he teaches me to be cool."

The future is radiantly bright for Grant. He has begun working with a new medium. He's making a cross out of beads and jewelry items. His calendar pieces are being made into cards and prints. Grant will be traveling to autism conferences and art shows, carrying his message, "It's not what we *can't* do, it's what we *can* do."

What started a little over a year ago as a way to supplement his home-school curriculum has turned into a blossoming business. It is all possible because of a mother who "found his genius" and never gave up on him. Julie still works with other children with autism, advocating on behalf of their careers in art, in addition to her own protégé. Grant is sure she will make a difference in their lives as she has in his, "She is incredible. I would not be here if she had not believed in me. My mom is my inspiration." Julie admits she's his biggest fan, "He just takes it all in stride. He's like, 'can we get something to eat?' I'm the one going crazy, jumping and cheering." No doubt Julie will be jumping a great deal in the future as Grant's stardom and his compassion continue to soar.

*For more information about Grant's Eco Art, you can visit his website at GrantsEcoArt.com.*

## TWO YEARS LATER

Grant's "COOLages" continue to bring him recognition and prestigious awards. He was named Austin's Rodeo Eco-Art Grand Champion two years in a row; he won the Bayou City Art Festival's New Emerging Artist Award this year; he won this year's High School Congressional award from the 8th District of Texas and was recognized for his artistic achievements by the Texas State Senate. His mother continues to marvel with pride at his accomplishments.

# Valerie Haines

## Nine Special Needs Children and an Incredible Mom

There are special people in this world and then there are EXTREMELY special people. Home health nurse Valerie Haines ranks right at the top of the heap!

Valerie, 50, has no children of her own but has enjoyed every second of her life as an adoptive mother to nine. Each child entrusted to her loving care has had a special health or developmental issue. The needs of her darlings range in severity. She has buried four of her precious children. The remaining five are quite a handful.

Valerie didn't wake up one day and decide to adopt children with disabilities or health issues. Many times it started with a phone call from Child Protective Services telling her about a special needs child with no one to care for him or her. Her first child, however, was born into her family. When Valerie was 12, her oldest brother and his wife gave birth to Jamey. This adorable, curly haired baby was born with holoprosencephaly, which means the brain doesn't divide. His was a severe case. He was never independent. He never learned to walk or talk but he communicated with his beautiful, hazel-colored eyes. Valerie fell in love him the first time she laid eyes on him. The pre-teen spent every minute she could with her beloved nephew. After she graduated from college, she adopted him and cared for him until he passed away in his sleep at the age of 19.

"The radiologist said it was amazing he was alive," recalls Valerie. "But he was such a joy. Every day he woke up smiling and he went to bed smiling. We were so close in age, he was able to experience being a kid through me. If I played football or went down a slide, he went with me."

Jamey wasn't going to remain an only child for long. Valerie was working on a pediatric floor at a nearby hospital when a baby was brought in with hydranencephaly. Baby Joshua only had a brain stem—the rest was fluid. Doctors predicted he would live only a few weeks. His biological mother had given him up before he was born and the waiting adoptive family didn't want him when they learned of his health issues. The only option left was to place him in a hospice facility to wait for him to die. Valerie couldn't let that happen. Of all her children, Joshua Ryan was the only child she was able to name (the rest came to her already named). "He had a very distinct, handsome face," says the proud mom. "I always thought if I laid eyes on the father I'd know him. He looked like a little man with a very beautiful face." Her "chunky monkey" with the enlarged head was eventually given a shunt in his brain. And despite his severe disabilities, he lived until three weeks shy of his third birthday.

Thirteen months after Joshua passed away, Jamey joined him in Heaven. Valerie decided she was done. But then, maybe not. Four months after Jamey died, Child Protective Services called Valerie and asked if she could take on a child with a litany of problems. Laycee (soon-to-be child number three) had oxygen depravation, heart defects, and was on a feeding tube at the time. Valerie told the case worker "no." When she told her mother about Laycee and her needs, Valerie's mother asked the simple question, "Who else is gonna do it?" Valerie headed to Dallas to pick her up.

Laycee was born with a congenital diaphragmatic hernia. Her diaphragm didn't form so her lungs and heart weren't developing properly, which made it difficult for her to breathe. Her survival rate was estimated at 20 percent. Laycee was put on a heart/lung bypass machine and she remained on it for 21 days. During that time doctors fixed her hernia but she suffered a massive stroke that destroyed a huge portion of the left side of her brain. "There wasn't a whole lot of hope. She couldn't do a whole lot," remembers Valerie. "She was four months old and it was a roller coaster ride. But she just turned eighteen and graduated from high school." Laycee is a beautiful, sensitive child who can read and draw and, even though she has suffered severe brain damage, she has a keen understanding of people. She can sense what people need—if they're sad or hurting. She is a whiz on the computer. One day she drew a picture of a face and the word got out about her talent. She has done portraits and sold them to customers in Canada, Netherlands and of course, here in the U.S. "What she wants to do is make the whole world smile," brags Valerie.

A few years later, Child Protective Services called again. They had a baby who had been born with a hypoplastic right heart. Joshua John ("I almost didn't take him because his name was Joshua") was on the way home with Valerie, when she realized something wasn't quite right. Joshua is severely autistic in addition to his heart condition. He was a lovable, fun little tyke. The protocol for a condition like Joshua's, calls for three surgeries over the course of about five years to correct the heart defect. He sailed through his first two and Valerie wanted to stop. He was thriving when no one thought he would live past a few months. When he first came to Valerie, he had been on mega-steroids. He was large and very hairy. "He looked like a blob," recalls Valerie. "I got out the razor and when I was through he looked like a doll." He hadn't received a lot of attention prior to joining Valerie's brood. But with loving and nurturing care, he was able to walk by the time he was 3. She finally agreed to let the doctors perform the final the surgery, which was successful. But tragically, Joshua passed away from a staph infection following the surgery not long after his 5th birthday.

Joshua and Laycee welcomed brother Adrian (number five) during Joshua's short time on this earth. This child had been diagnosed with interstitial lung disease and suffered from chronic lung problems and infections. He was oxygen dependent and tube fed. He was two and took

17 medications a day. Now he's thriving under Valerie's efficient and loving care and requires minimal meds. He is now a teenager.

Adrian has dark skin, hair and eyes. "He is my sweet soul. He will do anything in the world to help me," Valerie says with a smile. "He is always there. He's very smart—not necessarily academically—but he's a very sweet soul and will help anyone with anything." Adrian is still tube fed at night. Laycee fixes his formula and he hooks himself up.

Child number six came much the same way the first arrived in her life. Her older brother had a son who ended up in Valerie's nest not long after Adrian. Michael was seven weeks old when she took him in and adopted him. He has a strong family history of bi-polar disorder, and exhibits many behaviors on the autism spectrum. Eleven-year-old Michael didn't do well in the mainstream school setting, becoming withdrawn and struggled to learn. And as if she didn't have enough on her plate, the traveling nurse decided to begin home-schooling Michael and Adrian. "Michael has a tender heart but is the most challenging because of behavioral issues," says Valerie. "He takes everything to heart. There's a lot more emotion with him than any other children. You have to use a different approach to keep from harming his soul." Michael looks the most like his mother—strawberry blond hair, blue eyes. While part of him wants to fit in with the rest of his siblings, Valerie says he feels a special connection since they share the same eye color.

Not long after she lost Joshua John, Valerie got another call. Arianna (lucky number seven) needed a home. This tiny little spitfire has no large intestine. She suffered from an ischemic bowel and doctors removed her colon at a very early age. She is now 7 years old and in first grade. Several times a year she'll have bacterial overgrowth and need IV fluids. She suffers from chronic diarrhea. She's a tomboy, "hard-headed, nothing fazes this child," laughs Valerie. "She's going to do what she wants to do. She's a beautiful girl who gets away with more than she should," according to her besotted mother, "She's just so stinking cute!"

Alexandra (they call her Xandra) was born at 25 weeks. The preemie had a grade three bleed on the left side of her brain and a grade four on the right. The brain damage was extensive. Naturally, Valerie couldn't say no to this child, who had been diagnosed as severely autistic on top of her neurological concerns. Xandra is a funny child with a cute laugh who loves to tease her sister Arianna. She can't carry on a conversation but she can repeat anything she's ever heard. The 7-year-old can hear simple notes and play them back on the piano though she's never been taught how to play. She keeps touching the keys until she figures out the right ones and can play the song. She is currently in a program for the severely handicapped and doing extremely well.

Last, but certainly not least, is Joseph (number nine). Joseph had been shot in a domestic dispute that left him with severe brain damage. He lost all the frontal lobe of his brain. Valerie fostered him for several years until Laycee became critically ill with a bowel obstruction. For four months Laycee was in intensive care and Valerie couldn't watch over Joseph. He was placed in a facility in Texas. Two years ago, Joseph came up for adoption. A caseworker, visiting Valerie to finalize Xandra's adoption, told her that Joseph needed a home. The next month he returned to Valerie and both adoptions (Xandra and Joseph) were soon finalized. He suffered violent seizures as a result of his childhood trauma. But when he wasn't in the throes of one, he was a gloriously happy child. He was a handsome, freckle-faced child with green eyes and red hair. "He was cute as a bug, always smiling. He was into everything!" At the age of 12, one of those seizures took Joseph's life.

The old woman in the shoe obviously has nothing on Valerie Haines. She modestly downplays the saintly, selfless lifestyle she has chosen. "To be honest, I don't know anything else. This is all I've ever done," says Valerie. Being a registered nurse has certainly helped Valerie with the many needs of her children. She admits there were times she felt overwhelmed. "I can remember vividly when I took Laycee straight out of ICU and brought her home. She was still on the bypap machine to help her breathe. She was tube fed and had an iliostomy that leaked constantly. My goal was to keep her comfortable. One day I couldn't get her bag to stop leaking," recalls Valerie. "I went to the back of the house and screamed. Then I went back and took care of her. It was so frustrating to see her hurt and I couldn't fix it."

Valerie is a home health nurse which works with her crazy life schedule. Laycee goes with Valerie to work because her health is so fragile. But Laycee also has her own role in the mostly-elderly visits. "All the patients wait for her. She hugs them, talks to them and listens to what they have to say. She is much better therapy (for the patients) than I am."

A lot of people tell Valerie these children are very blessed. "But I feel like I'm the one blessed. I can't imagine life without them. It's such a privilege to be their parent and to see the things they can do that no one thought they could ever do. When I went to the hospital to get Laycee at four months old, a resident in the neo-natal program came up to me and, unsolicited, told me to 'have fun with that one. All she's gonna do is stare at the walls.'" Valerie says with clenched teeth. "The door shut before I could get to him. All I could think was, 'how DARE HE! How could he take away her future like that?' If I didn't know any better, I might have believed him. How tragic that people look at children like her and say things like that. My children all have potential and something to give. Whether it's a smile or artwork or becoming a doctor one day, they can do something! We have to have expectations. If we expect nothing, we get nothing. With all my children, I set goals they can reach. I look at each one of them and see what they can accomplish and be proud of.

"I haven't adopted every (special needs) child that I've come across. With each child in my life, I knew it was right. I knew it was already predestined they'd end up with me. It was already set."

Is nine enough for this Super Mom? Well, she recently got another call.

## TWO YEARS LATER

Valerie reports that, for the most part, things are status quo. Laycee is beginning to struggle more with health issues. They just take each day as it comes. The boys are GROWING! Adrian is now 5'6" and Michael is not far behind him. "It is funny to see them standing next to Laycee who is 20 and stands 4'6" tall," says Valerie. The little girls are thriving. Xandra was placed in a special program for autistic children and impresses the teachers with her talent. Arianna is now in third grade and is doing very well. Mother Extraordinaire, Valerie, continues to work from home so that she can stay with Laycee and provide the constant care and supervision she needs.

# Jaundice: *NEVER TAKE IT LIGHTLY*

## David Powell's Mother on a Mission

The beautiful David Powell entered our world a healthy, full-term, robust Caesarean baby who aced his newborn Apgar test. His parents, Sarahann and Jacob, were a typical new mom and dad team—proud, joyous and completely in awe of their precious, first-born child.

The first inkling that something was amiss was evident in just a few hours. David didn't want to wake up.

It took two nurses, stripping him to the diaper, using cold washcloths to wake him up to feed. His bilirubin, a welcome 6.9 (ten is normal with newborns) gave no indication of what David was about to experience. Even though the red flags were raging, the Powells were discharged and told to see his pediatrician two days later. By that time, his bilirubin was a terrifying 32.4.

Once those labs came in, David was rushed to the hospital where the level rose even higher to 39.8. He was put under phototherapy (the blue lights) with the hopes of breaking down the bilirubin.

With these devastating numbers, the local doctors had him transferred to the children's hospital at the Medical University of South Carolina. There, he underwent two double volume exchange blood transfusions. At a very slow rate, David's blood was drained out and new blood replaced it to try to bring his numbers down. But his liver just wasn't working. The bilirubin, which acts like a poison, had already attacked David's infant brain. "We now know David has a G6PB deficiency," says Sarahann. "It's a blood enzyme deficiency. In most people it's not life threatening. It reacts to food and certain medications. Everybody has this enzyme." The G6PB protects white blood cells. When a person lacks this, the white blood cells have no protection. If they come in contact with certain foods and drugs, the white blood cells start bursting because they have nothing to protect them. This can eventually cause anemia. "David had been anemic a couple of times but nothing major. One of the medications he was given was the vitamin K injection given to all newborns to prevent blood clots. When they gave him the shot, his body reacted to it and shut down his liver," recalls Sarahann. "That's why the bilirubin shot up and the jaundice set in."

It didn't take long for the doctors to diagnose David with Kernicterus. It's a "fancy name for brain damage caused by excessive bilirubin," says the now all-too-informed mother. There are a whole array of symptoms that Kernicterus patients can experience—blindness, auditory neuropathy and eventually, many of these children are diagnosed with Cerebral Palsy.

David has not been diagnosed with CP as of the publication of this article. He received a neuromuscular dysfunction diagnosis. He has several CP characteristics—athetosis (uncontrolled movement), spasticity (spastic muscle movements) and hyper and hypotonicity (in some parts of his body the muscles are less toned and others they are increased). David has very little stomach and arm muscle strength but his legs are extremely toned. He can barely bend his legs; sometimes they seem almost locked.

Developmentally, David is delayed. He has trouble speaking. He babbles and communicates on the level of about a one-year-old, according to his mother. At two, David has just started walking but is still about a year behind otherwise. One of his conditions is extreme drooling. A swallowing study showed that this was causing chronic congestion and cough, which has led to chronic lung issues. He is on an inhaler.

David underwent a successful procedure to correct his extreme acid reflux (GERD). The procedure wrapped his stomach around his esophagus to strengthen the sphincter muscles to prevent acid from getting to his esophagus.

In January, David received a cochlear implant to address the damage to his auditory nerve. Doctors hope this will speed up his speech development as his hearing improves.

The Powells address each and every procedure, therapy and symptom systematically. Sarahann researches her child's condition(s) and advocates for his treatments. There are only one or two cases of Kernicterus in most states. It is such a rare condition, the parents have been forced to become the experts. "The doctors know how to treat the side effects, but not necessarily the overall cause. David sees an array of specialists," says Sarahann. "I have to remind the ENT that his problems are not only his ears. His speech delay is not necessarily auditory. He has jaw weakness. The muscles in his face are affected by neurological dysfunction. We have to remind the audiologist that there are other reasons he has hearing problems. Some doctors have never even heard of Kernicterus and they certainly haven't ever treated someone with it."

Sarahann enlists the help of family members to help her with David's care. She has a cousin in Florence, South Carolina, who is a pediatrician and she helps clarify the medications and the diagnoses. A sister-in-law, Tiffany Powell, works at another pediatric office and is also a valuable resource. Tiffany gives Sarahann all the credit for David's many successes, "They said he wouldn't be able to hear. She was told of a lot of things that she wasn't going to let happen. I'm not sure where he would be right now if it wasn't for her pushing for therapies—physical and speech therapies. Everything she does, day in and day out, is for him. We look at him and we're amazed he can say some words. Now he's had this surgery so he can be able to hear and hopefully speak. She does so much for him. It's amazing. She lives to make sure that boy can do what he needs to do."

"David is a little boy with a lot of problems," says Sarahann. "This cochlear implant was a big decision. We didn't know if his problems were auditory or muscular. Now we wait and see if eventually the speech catches up. He's in several therapies like oral motor therapy for his mouth weaknesses. We'll see if the implant helps. With auditory neuropathy, the nerves that run from the cochlea to the brain have issues transmitting the information. What he hears doesn't sound like what you and I hear. It's very distorted; it can come and go. It's like a staticky radio station and could go from normal to muted in an instant." The implant will hopefully stimulate the nerve and help it rejuvenate to control the quality and consistency of sound David is hearing.

When David was first transferred to the children's hospital where he received the transfusions, he had his first seizure. More would follow. The seizures (a telltale sign that the body's in distress) started causing apnea. An EEG confirmed the problems were neurological and after an MRI, it was evident that there was brain damage. "I remember the neurologist calling it an area of suspicion. At that point my husband and I hadn't had enough education about jaundice being a danger," recalls Sarahann. "We were still clueless. It took days for the doctors to determine that jaundice was the cause of David's brain damage. We thought 'Jaundice? No big deal.' But it's a huge deal."

David passed the auditory test given with his newborn screening. But within the month (after suffering severe jaundice and after the Kernicterus diagnosis), he failed the same test twice.

David's condition has brought out the raging advocate in Sarahann. She has joined a support group called PICK (Parents of Infants and Children with Kernicterus, pickonline.org) and now serves on its board. Her goal (other than to care for her precious child) is to educate the community about jaundice and its devastating potential. "We didn't take it lightly but it still affected him. We don't want this to happen to any other child. David is considered a very mild case. Most kids' (Cerebral Palsy) symptoms are so extreme, they're wheelchair bound and never speak. We're very lucky the bilirubin was brought down so quickly, thanks to the doctors and because we knew it was serious." David's prognosis is extremely positive.

Kernecteris, sadly, is 98 percent preventable. David's case, because it advanced so rapidly, wasn't preventable. But the outcome could have been much worse. Sarahann's mission is to make every parent aware of the hazards of jaundice and to *never take it lightly*. Her sister-in-law, Tiffany, shares her passion, "We have babies come to the office with jaundice. We have to call the parents to get them back in for a recheck. They don't want to put their baby under the lights. These parents just don't understand what can happen if their child reaches high levels—that brain damage can happen. It's sad because they don't realize they could damage their child for the rest of his life."

When parents refuse treatment for their child's jaundice, Tiffany tells them about David and, if she has to, brings in the big guns: Sarahann.

Sarahann has printed cards with her name and number on them and has left them in doctor's offices throughout the Charleston area. She is always available to talk to any parent who either doesn't take jaundice seriously or whose child may already have suffered its effects. She is currently writing a book about David and his story. Tiffany says it will be a great tool for pediatricians and parents, "It's a book about a person who went through this. It can open people's eyes. If I wasn't in the medical field, I wouldn't know about jaundice. My first son had jaundice and we put him under the lights. The doctors wouldn't let him go until the jaundice was taken care of. Until I got into medical field, I didn't realize it was such a big deal.

A pamphlet made by Sarahann—an actual person—is a big deal. She's a real live person this happened to."

In the meantime, David is Sarahann's number one concern. "He's a normal child with some issues that we're dealing with. Hopefully when he gets older he won't have these issues. We're tackling them while he's young so that he can live the most productive life possible."

"No matter how much is going on with her, she's always willing to go that extra step," says Tiffany. "She's always the caregiver. She does what she needs to do to make sure everyone else is okay before she thinks about herself. That's what makes her who she is."

And Sarahann is a mom on a mission: "The word needs to get out there that jaundice is not a simple problem that will go away. If you ignore it, it will creep up on you and become a big issue. I don't think many people understand just how serious jaundice is."

## TWO YEARS LATER

Since the article was written, David Powell, now five-years-old, received a unilateral cochlear implant. It provides him with a consistent, good quality of sound that he otherwise would not be receiving due to his auditory neuropathy. He started school when he turned 3. He is in a hearing impaired auditory verbal classroom for the third year this year and is doing great. His vocabulary has flourished and he is making wonderful progress. Physically, David is progressing as well. He struggles with balance issues and falls a lot. He played his first season of t-ball in the spring and is now playing soccer and loves every minute of it. While he realizes he can't do things as well as the other children, he works very hard and never gives up.

# Her Middle Name is *Hope*
## Katie and Lilah's Story

From the first moment Katie looked at her beautiful fourth baby, she knew something was wrong. "They told me it was the goo they put in babies' eyes. I knew better," recalls Katie. "Something is wrong with her eyes." Baby Lilah Hope was also having trouble breathing. For several frightening hours the staff struggled with Lilah's respiratory issues. Finally, once the baby was stable, Katie was able to ask about the milky film that appeared to encase her child's eyes. Her pediatrician, Dr. Robert Cosio, saw it too.

Lilah's eyes couldn't reflect light. Her eyes were almost completely white. Katie couldn't see the colors of her iris or pupil because they were so clouded. A consultation with a local pediatric opthamologist was recommended.

At just 18 hours old, Lilah had her eyes poked and scraped and wedged open. Katie was told to hold her now-screaming child. After what felt like a brutal assault on her tiny baby, the doctor announced that he didn't have good news. Katie recalls his next words, which were forever seared into her heart. "He said, 'God didn't make these eyes right. You're at the beginning of an extremely long road. She will need bi-corneal transplants.'" He went on to warn her that the transplants would cause glaucoma. "He told me, 'at best, she will have one eye.' And then he walked out of the room." Lilah's father, Aaron, remembers that day all too well, "The thought of my newborn daughter having to go through such a procedure was incredibly scary and the possibility of her being blind was terrifying."

This diagnosis is a far cry from the successful, *seeing* child that Lilah is today.

A "wonderful" (as Katie describes him every time he's mentioned) corneal specialist, Dr. William Barry Lee, was consulted on Lilah's specific condition. He first saw her when she was four weeks old, just two days before Christmas 2008. At first, Dr. Lee favored transplants as the direction they needed to take. Then he stopped. He remembered several patients who had improved from similar conditions just using steroid drops in the eyes. Katie said she and Aaron gratefully decided to at least try the drops before going any further. That day, the Sharps went to the pharmacy, got the steroid drops and, "held that bottle in our hands and prayed, PLEASE GOD, let this *work*!" They shook the bottle, put the drops in her eyes and drove home.

A week later, they returned to Dr. Lee's office for an evaluation and his first words to the Sharps were, "I have never seen a child's eyes clear this fast. I don't know what you're doing but keep doing it." Katie says it was prayer: "We prayed for the doctor. We prayed for these drops and we prayed that God would guide her and heal her." Dr. Lee told them to come back in three weeks. Every visit after that, a part of her eye would be clearer than the last visit and the haze was getting thinner. At around seven months, Dr. Lee determined that Lilah suffered from Peter's Anomoly in her right eye and sclero cornea in her left eye. That's when Dr. Lee announced that sclero cornea patients do not transplant well. The Sharps are grateful for the steroid drops and grateful they waited before proceeding with the transplants.

Lilah has come such a long way from the child doctors predicted would never see. She now has 20/80 vision. She's truly a miracle. At 22 months, she was tested for a possible genetic abnormality. While waiting for those results, Katie simply enjoyed the progress Lilah made and was taking it one day at a time. "She is learning to babble and say, 'Mama and Dada,'" says the proud Katie. "She's definitely an observer. Though she couldn't see in the beginning, she now watches you and pays attention and imitates those gestures later on. She is just learning to cruise. She will only walk a few steps with her medical walker but at least she's walking. She wears AFOs (an orthotic brace) to give her lower legs and feet stability and strength."

The Sharps' strength throughout Lilah's development has come from a deep faith in God. They're grateful for the help that came from a team of local agencies that have been advocates who provide invaluable medical and therapeutic resources. But, sadly, Katie didn't have this support system that horrible first day in the hospital. She had to search and reach out to find the people and agencies that are in place for families like hers. And she says it shouldn't have to be that way. "From the moment Lilah was diagnosed with this visual disability, we were left alone. I was in that hospital bed with this baby and no one came to talk to us except maybe a nurse here and there to do our vital signs," recalls Katie. "There were no social workers, no agency visits, nobody gave us a pamphlet about the agencies that are available. All they did, was basically say, 'Here you go. Your child's different.' Nobody even said, 'I'm sorry, what can I do?'"

Lilah was five months old before Katie learned about Babies Can't Wait (an early intervention program sponsored by Part C of the Individuals with Disabilities Education Act). Once Katie and Lilah were admitted to the program, they learned about physical, occupational and even speech therapies that have been crucial in Lilah's success. It was Babies Can't Wait staff that told Katie about Georgia Pines—a (Georgia) state initiative for visually and hearing impaired children—an invaluable advocate for parents. At five months, Lilah was just lying on her back. She wasn't doing anything developmentally. She had no motivation to roll for a toy because she didn't have the vision to see the object. Her ever-searching mom learned later that the Savannah Association for the Blind offers a preschool service for visually impaired children. It wasn't until Katie's first visit with Babies Can't Wait that Katie learned her child needed to be evaluated for possible inclusion in all these advocacy/prevention programs. "I think when she was diagnosed, nobody knew what to say," says Katie. "I think people were afraid to tell me the truth. But I just wish someone would have reassured us. They could have suggested she might be delayed and recommended that we seek out these services. Nobody gave me a list and said, 'Here are the people you should call.' No social worker ever called. There was no follow-through from the hospital. Somebody dropped the ball.

"I know there are parents like us, who don't even know about Georgia Pines. Many don't know about Babies Can't Wait. I know there are parents who don't even know about services at Savannah Association for the Blind (or similar agencies in other cities and communities). The doctors and the therapists seem to know how to help you more when you're in an advocate's care. They can open your eyes to things. There should be pamphlets in every doctor's office. When a child is diagnosed as different or delayed, someone in that office should hand that parent a pamphlet that has lists and telephone numbers of all the agencies, the hospitals, and everything neatly compiled for assistance with every spectrum. Then parents will know they're not alone. If I had known there was somebody out there, I probably could have done more for Lilah."

The Sharps have and continue to be their daughter's biggest advocate. Katie consistently researches Lilah's condition and symptoms on the internet and has started a blog called Lilah's Hope. In that blog, she solicits ideas and solutions to Lilah's issues; she asks for prayers and she shares her story with others who might be beginning a similar journey.

After Lilah's needs are under control and there's a little more time in Katie's life, (she's also a freelance photographer on the side—katiesharpphotography@gmail.com), she hopes to develop resources that will connect new families of special needs children with the proper agency. The Sharps still aren't sure if, in their situation, they simply "fell through the cracks" or if they were overlooked because of Lilah's specific, rare condition, but they hope one day to help others. Katie's already started meeting with support groups and soliciting agency information so that no one ever has to feel abandoned in a hospital room.

Katie has become an inspiration not only to her family but also to those who are privileged to work with her and her precious child on a day-to-day basis. Dawn Carter, special coordinator with Babies Can't Wait, describes Katie as a super-mom. "Katie has so many of the right qualities. She has high energy, great common sense, and she understands and learns. She researches, self advocates and educates herself tremendously. She does all of that while being a super involved mother, especially with those four children." Dawn says she's an inspiration, "I don't know how she does what she does. She's a multi-tasker. She's intelligent and uninhibited."

That multi-tasking trait comes in handy taking care of not just Lilah, but also Alex (7), Sammie (5) and Eli (3). Katie says it's important the entire family know what is going on at all times. "We have told them from the beginning that their sister was born different," says Katie. "I took a plastic cover that was opaque and I put it up to the girls' eyes. I said this is how Lilah sees. I explained things are different for her, and when they look at kids in a wheelchair, they should never stare. I remind them that they don't like it when people ask us unkind things about Lilah." The children have all been part of Lilah's life and part of her development. They've prayed and been part of prayer chains; they were on board when Lilah began the genetic testing and they've lived the rollercoaster that goes along with so many wait-and-see moments. They know all about MRI's and the different types of doctors and therapies. "I explain to them that God made her a little different. That doesn't mean she's wrong, doesn't mean she's not as good as them, she's just going to take a little bit longer to get her to where they are," says Katie. "When we're pregnant, we all pray for a certain baby. We pray for a child born with two arms, two legs, heart, kidneys.

You may not always get the child you pray for but you get the child you were meant to have. Lilah has taught my family so much about compassion, love and acceptance. Our family has a huge bond." The oldest, Alex, has a great "servant's heart." Sometimes on Saturday mornings, Alex will get Lilah out of her bed, change her diaper and make her laugh while their mom catches a few more moments of rest. Sammie just wants to love on her little sister, sometimes a little too much. She will pick Lilah up, kiss her, and then twirl Lilah around while Katie holds her breath that no one gets hurt. Eli is her protector. He comes over to his precious sister and puts his hand on her. He's the closest to Lila's age and he's been involved with all their therapies. He has seen firsthand how hard she works every day of every week. "I think it has made my children better human beings to have a special child in the family," says Katie.

"Those four children are going to be ahead of the game understanding that we're all individuals and we all have strengths," says Dawn. "They have an understanding that the activities done with this little girl are making a difference in how she becomes an independent child. They're learning things that people who go into early childhood education are learning. They're learning so much right now."

And for now, the family waits. They are waiting to hear the results of Lilah's genetic testing to see if there is yet another obstacle the family will have to overcome. "If she does have a rare genetic thing, it's not going to change her. I just want to know how to help her so I can hold her hand and guide her. And then some day, I can let go so she can do it on her own," says Katie. "I get so emotional. Some people judge her because her eyes turn and she doesn't look like everyone. They're missing so much. They're missing a relationship with this child who is the most beautiful, special, kind, funny, amazing little thing."

"She has been such a blessing. She's truly Heaven sent. She was a surprise baby, but she's priceless," brags proud dad, Aaron. "Everyone she meets is affected by her smile. You have to see it—you have to see her smile. She's the cutest thing. You have to meet her."

# TWO YEARS LATER

Lilah has made many remarkable strides. She is now walking independently with the help of her white cane that helps to aid her in depth perception and prepares her for what is coming next. She can communicate with four to five phrase sentences, loves music and can beat box better than most. When the article was first written two years ago, the family was waiting to hear about her genetic testing. They learned that she has a deletion on her 8th chromosome that explains her low tone and delay in process but she has happily conquered all the challenges warned about from that report. Lilah now has four older step-siblings who are as much a part of her life as her biological siblings. So, yes, she is the part of a blended family of ten. New husband, Randy, and Katie have known each other since high school and have merged what they call RK8 nicely. Lilah's therapists often praise her older seven siblings as daily therapists who help push Lilah to reach new heights. Lilah attends the Pre-K inclusion class at West Chatham and is exceeding her IEP goals every day. She took her first steps a few weeks after her 3rd birthday and is now RUNNING! Her mom believes "that God sent her to teach us all about love, perseverance, dedication, hard work, discipline and faith." Katie continues to advocate for many families with similar challenges. "God gave Lilah to me because He knew I would speak, shout, and share every valley and triumph—all that we have learned. I am blessed to be her Mama. She is my teacher."

# The Amazing, Inspirational Jennifer McGee
### Four Special Kids

She is a working mom with a high stress job. She's studying for her doctorate in counseling psychology. She has four active children; three of them have autism. And she's a tireless advocate for other parents of children with special needs.

Unbelievable? Amazing? Inspirational?

Yep. All of the above.

Her name is Jennifer McGee. She and her husband, Matthew, were blessed with Catherine (13), twins Connor and Carson (8) and Abby (7). The three older children are at different levels on the autism spectrum. Catherine is the most affected. She has Hypotonic Cerebral Palsy. She is G-tube fed, moderately intellectually disabled and is more developmentally delayed. Catherine reads on a third grade level and has severe social issues. Interaction with others is difficult for her because she doesn't speak well and is difficult to understand. She requires constant supervision for her safety and for assistance with daily needs.

Jennifer's twins, Connor and Carson, are higher functioning. The 8-year-olds are entering the third-grade with special support in the classroom. They have difficulty making friends and interacting with others, especially outside the family.

Abby, the youngest, is the typical 7-year-old. She's rambunctious and has proven to be a challenge in her own right, "because she actually talks back," laughs Jennifer.

Jennifer's personal experiences and her professional knowledge have made her the "go-to" person for parents of special needs children throughout this region.

Jennifer's undergraduate degree is in education with a major in speech language. She chose this path long before she gave birth to a special child of her own. "There's a definite amount of irony here. I think that's what enables me to do the trainings and be a mediator for families," says Jennifer. "Having been a professional first and familiar with the system gives me an insight. Other parents with, let's say, a degree in business would have to learn a whole new system and way of doing things. That's what helps me do my job. I have learned to communicate and understand others so needs are met."

Jennifer is an advocacy/education specialist at the Matthew Rearden Center for Autism, which is a facility dedicated to the needs of children with autism and their families. Her colleagues and her clients say she is a godsend. "Jennifer has volunteered to go with me to my son's school and sit in on our IEP (Individualized Education Plan) meetings and offer suggestions to his teachers," says Alicia Johnson (an appreciative parent). "She has also suggested that I take my son to a pediatric gastroenterologist to help him with his stomach issues. It just never dawned on his doctor to recommend that."

Matthew Rearden Center Executive Director Helen Waters agrees that Jennifer has that special gift that makes parents feel comfortable. "She gets the calls from parents of a child who has just been diagnosed," says Helen. "These parents see their hopes and dreams for that child altered dramatically. They are in an emotional state. Jennifer is calm, well spoken and basically unflappable. She helps them through, partly because of her professional expertise, but also because she's a mom with three children on the autism spectrum herself."

The IEP is daunting for new parents and Jennifer's job is to interpret this complex federal law and to negotiate and advocate on behalf of her clients (the parents and the child). Her role is to see that the law fully represents the child's best interest. She works to prevent any conflicts from forming an adversarial relationship between the parents and the education providers.

But that's not all she does for the Matthew Rearden Center. She also organizes workshops that bring speakers here from across the country who wouldn't normally come to Savannah. These are the experts in all fields related to special needs. Some of the topics involve organizational techniques and creating structure in the home. They may offer simple, practical tips that parents can take home with them and use that day.

Her boss says that of her many roles, however, Jennifer has her greatest impact when she interacts directly with the parents in that quiet, confident manner of hers. "It is very comforting and helpful to parents who know they are working with someone who is walking the walk," says Helen. "They may be at different stages. They may have just learned about their child. They may have hit a bump in the road. They may need help talking to their child's teacher. Whatever their need, it's such a comfort for them to work with someone so professionally well-versed, who understands what they're facing and knows how to handle whatever comes along. She's faced it all personally."

And "facing it" is what she has done and what she does every day. During her early months and years of motherhood with children with autism, Jennifer learned new ways to communicate with these hard-to-reach children. She learned how to operate a G-tube to nourish her first child, how to brush her child's ultra sensitive teeth, and how to find their potential in spite of their limitations. "Catherine likes to swim and to shop like a typical 13-year-old," laughs Jennifer. "She loves music. She has learned how to go on the computer and look them up on YouTube. She needs extra support in the classroom setting and is starting middle school this year. There aren't as many opportunities for her but she still manages to enjoy a lot of the things girls her age enjoys."

The twins have found their interest in a big way and it came about because of Jennifer's tireless determination. "We had tried to get the boys into Tae Kwon Do, but the director was hesitant about taking them both in his class," recalls Jennifer. "Their little sister, Abby, had been taking dance and they had been to her recital and loved it. When the boys said they wanted to try it, I asked the teacher if she would consider them and she agreed to take them on." Connor and Carson not only did well in dance, they thrived! The twins started participating in public performances that first year. Articles have been written about them in local magazines and newspapers. Other families of children with disabilities have signed up as well, and Jennifer has helped the teacher become better equipped to manage these children. Connor and Carson have competed nationally along with Abby, performing with the team in Orlando this year.

Jennifer has chosen to cut out much of the therapy programs for her children. "I didn't want them growing up in waiting rooms. I utilize my therapist friends. We have a pool in the back yard and a swing set," says Jennifer. "When my oldest needed to work on balance, we built a balance beam. We incorporated therapy into their play so they could focus on being kids."

The speech therapist comes to the house twice a week. Even though Jennifer's undergraduate background is in speech therapy, she says she doesn't "sit around and do speech therapy" with her kids. "I know I want more spontaneous language and I know how to incorporate that into bath and dinnertime. I pick goals to work on at home. I use structure and organization to promote independence in them."

Some of Jennifer's tricks include visual references. The boys' dressers have pictures of what goes into each drawer. They're learning how to fold laundry and put it away and they have learned to get dressed in the morning on their own. Catherine didn't start walking until age three. Jennifer pasted pictures of a gold fish on the container at the bottom of the refrigerator. When Catherine wanted that favorite snack, she would crawl over to the goldfish picture and point to it. Every form of communication was a success for the children. Every step toward independence was another victory.

Jennifer is quick to acknowledge the "tag team" that helps make her life run so smoothly. She and her husband, Matthew, have a running joke, "We hear the divorce rate is higher with twins and higher if the parents have children with autism. So, technically, we shouldn't be talking to one another," she laughs. "Seriously, we have to work together, not only to manage our family but for each of us to pursue our own personal interests." Jennifer's personal interest was to return to school to earn her doctorate. That required more time from Matthew and more juggling. He officiates high school wrestling. It takes regular family meetings to schedule each other's activities, especially now that the children are older and have their own events that require parental help and involvement. "Carson played football last year. He had difficulty understanding the game so my husband had to be there," said Jennifer. "Matthew had to help the coaches help Carson figure out how to play. He did learn to tackle the person with the ball but he doesn't understand what the rest of the players are doing on the field. So, they made him a safety and he knew to tackle. That was a way to find what works for him."

Besides Matthew, Jennifer is blessed to have the support of her parents and her sister who all live gloriously nearby. Those family members are quick to babysit or to carpool the children to activities. Jennifer and her children have been such an inspiration that her sister, Joanna Hint, went back to school to learn Applied Behavioral Analysis therapy and also works with children with special needs and their families. "Jennifer and her children have made me a better person. I don't take anything for granted now," says Joanna. "Life is about the moment—each and every small moment. It's not just about the big picture. These children live in the 'right now' and how 'right now' affects them. They don't think about a week later. They don't worry about things that could hurt them or benefit them later in life. Those little rewards they show me, every little sign of progression, that's what keeps me going. Those little rewards make it all worth it."

Jennifer's always-understanding boss works with her crazy schedule and that flexibility helps Jennifer meet her children's and her clients' needs. "She amazes me that with all she has going on at home, she will tell us, 'If someone calls for me, give them my cell number,'" says Helen.

Joanna sees every day what her sister means to these parents, "A lot of parents are lost until they meet Jennifer. She starts advising them and they know she has the education background. Then they find out she lives it at home every day! They gravitate to her and trust her."

The Matthew Rearden Center cites many success stories thanks to Jennifer and other devoted staff members like her. One graduate from the program is now a student at Savannah Tech and volunteers at Effingham hospital. "That's what I like to see," says Jennifer proudly. "The parents of this young man are ecstatic about his accomplishment. I love it when the parents of the young children with severe behaviors are aiming higher for their kids. It's not always like that. Some parents of special needs children are geared to aim low. We need to reverse that. We need to let these children rise to the occasions. We will be surprised what they can do given the appropriate support and the right opportunities.

"I want both professionals and parents to start seeing children in a positive light. When you talk about autism, ask about the growing numbers. Talk to parents and find out about their struggles because of lack of resources and lack of money. But, on the other side, so much focus is on what children *can't* do and what's *not* available for them. Very few stories celebrate the successes of these children. We need more awareness of what they can do with the appropriate support so they can be successful. Look at what the children can do at the dance studio. That studio had no experience with children with special needs, but they took a chance and were very successful and now they are an example to other organizations. They can open doors and provide opportunities.

"My children have been a huge influence on me and the decision I made about myself and my future and how I look at the world. Catherine has been my greatest teacher. I feel I am better person because of her and her brothers and sister. If you'd have asked me 15 years ago what my profession would have been, it would have never been like this," admits Jennifer.

Many, like Alicia Johnson, are grateful to Jennifer and the road she's traveled, "She can truly relate to parents of children with any disability, especially autism. I do and have recommended her to friends. Jennifer is someone I plan to keep in our lives for a very long time. She is amazing!"

## TWO YEARS LATER

Catherine McGee is now 17 and attends high school. She continues to make progress and is developing work related skills. Her favorite things are listening to music, YouTube, and going to the beach! Connor and Carson McGee are now 12 years old and have entered middle school. This has been a major adjustment and learning experience for everyone involved, especially their mom! They continue to work on academics, learn how to interact with other peers, and become more independent! Connor is playing the trombone for 6th grade band and Carson plans to try out for the wrestling team. Abby is now 10 and continues to grow into her own person. She has begun some modeling and commercial work. However, her love continues to be dance where she competes across the southeast. Jennifer McGee continues to work for The Matthew Reardon Center for Autism as their Advocacy/Education Specialist. She is also a Licensed Professional Counselor with a small practice in Pooler where she offers individual and family counseling, as well as social skill therapy groups for elementary to high school aged children. She is currently a doctoral candidate, completing her dissertation on mental health professional's view of autism.

# A Canine Companion
## Nykiah's Helper

Nykiah and her twin sister, Nykayla, were born two months early and each weighed less than two pounds. Their mother, Paula, had suffered five miscarriages before their remarkable births. Bringing them into the world wasn't easy. The doctors discovered fibroids in Paula's uterus during the pregnancy. When she was five months along, there were complications and she was hospitalized for two months. After the twins were born, it didn't take long to realize that Nykiah might not live the normal life that Nykayla would enjoy.

Nykiah was diagnosed with Cerebral Palsy and fitted with a wheelchair as soon as her ambulatory limitations were fully realized. She also has limited use of her hands. While she loves to draw and play at her kitchen table, she is prone to drop things and requires help retrieving the fallen items. Paula says it seemed like a full-time job, just keeping up with the many pencils, crayons and toys that were scattered at the base of Nykiah's wheelchair.

Then, one night Paula was watching a show featuring former vice presidential candidate Sarah Palin (the mother of a child with Down syndrome) and a little boy with CP. His parents had acquired a canine companion to help him. The intelligent dog picked up the many pencils the child dropped and would dutifully give them back to its charge. "I heard them say, 'for more information,'" recalls Paula. "I ran downstairs to get on the computer." That was April 2010. The optimistic mother filled out an application and was jubilant to hear from the organization four days later. She filled out the extensive application about their family. She shared her hopes for the dog and its benefit to her child and mailed the application. Soon she was contacted to travel to Orlando for a personal interview and to meet with a dog and trainer.

By the end of July, the family received the news that they'd been approved for a canine companion. The four of them traveled to Orlando for two weeks of extensive training the next month. After working with several dogs, Nykiah was matched with Carol, a beautiful golden retriever mix with loving eyes and fearless loyalty. "Nykiah loves that dog. She drops a pencil. I give the command for Carol to get it. Carol can hand it to Nykiah. Kids used to look at Nykiah and stare. They used to ask us why Nykiah was in the wheelchair. Now that Carol is with us, they look at the dog."

For the first 30 days of her training, no one was allowed to touch or interact with Carol except Paula and Nykiah. There was a touch of jealousy from Nykayla after the long training period in Orlando from which she was excluded. Afterward, to top it all off, now there was a dog in the house that was exclusively Nykiah's. Nykayla was feeling left out but she had Brandon (the family dog) and the family made peace by designating Brandon Nykayla's dog.

Carol is like any working or therapy animal. When she's on duty she's all business. When she's off duty, she can be a pet. She's tirelessly devoted to her young charge. When she sees the wheelchair moving, she jumps up and finds her position to the left of the chair. She is able to follow 37 commands. She can push the handicap button on electric doors. She knows what to pick up and how to give it to Nykiah. "It's meant the world to her. She feels like she has something of her own," says Paula. "A lot of times they have friends come over to play. These children can walk and run. The girls will play with Nykiah at the table but understandably, they get tired of sitting after a while. They want to run around and often leave Nykiah by herself. She doesn't feel as bad as she had in the past." Nykiah is never alone anymore because she always has Carol by her side.

Nykayla's initial resentment over the special dog was short-lived. Now she's happy her twin has Carol. "It makes Nykiah happy because Carol's nice to her," Nykayla says with a smile. "When we tell our other dog to do something, he doesn't do it. Carol does. She's so smart and so well-behaved." Nykiah says Carol is fun: "We play teacher. We dress up. We dance. Mommy tells Carol what to do and she takes care of me."

Paula hopes Carol will be around a long time. She knows young people in college who have a companion dog and she knows it provides independence and security. Carol will retire at around the age of ten, which is less than eight years from now. As far as the family's concerned (and especially the very grateful parents), Carol is not going anywhere. "We're gonna keep that dog," says Paula. "She's part of the family."

# TWO YEARS LATER

Carol the "working canine" is four years old now and she has far exceed the expectations of her owners. Nykiah and Paula are currently teaching Carol how to retrieve drinks out of the refrigerator for her precious mistress. Nykiah is doing GREAT in middle school-making As and Bs. She still loves her Carol but spends up a lot of time on her laptop. Nykala is a cheerleader at a charter school in Savannah and enjoys it. Nykiah was recently diagnosed with scoliosis and faces back surgery. Paula is confident Carol will be by her daughter's side through it all. Since the dog has become part of their family, Nykiah has been much happier and more accepted and felt more like a normal kid among her peers. The family prays for many more years with Carol in their lives.

# Kim and Patrick Spencer
## Advocate Mom and her Special Son

Patrick Spencer was a few months shy of three years old when he was diagnosed with Pervasive Developmental Disorder (PDD). Kim Spencer was pregnant with Patrick's sister, Anna Brooke, when she made a terrifying discovery related to this diagnosis.

The signs had been painfully apparent since his early months. A woman once described a tantrum of Patrick's at eight months as "bi-polar." He exhibited super-human strength for a child so young. It took three adults to hold him down for a haircut and the screams could be heard more than a few houses away. He once kicked Kim in the head so violently she had to have a CT scan. Several times, her efforts to control him hurt her back. Kim had to strap him down to brush his teeth and hair. He was extremely loving and extremely violent. He knew all his colors, shapes, letters and numbers at 18 months. He also knew labels. He could point out any object and tell you what it's called but could not form a sentence. That inability to communicate was the key to his diagnosis and it was a speech pathologist who broke the news of the Pervasive Development Disorder to his shocked mother. "I looked at her and said 'how dare you label my child?'" Kim recalls. "For the next eight hours, I was furious. When I couldn't go to sleep that night, I googled PDD and saw what it means. It means *autism*."

That sleepless night spent on the internet sparked Kim's plan of action. She read about the effects of wheat and dairy on a child's behavior. "He ate seven things at that time and they were all wheat and dairy. I took them away the next day. He had a 10-hour withdrawal period like coming off heroin. In three days he finally saw me for the first time."

For the next two and a half years, Kim searched and researched any and all avenues to learn more about this elusive condition. She found Yahoo groups and reference books and, with her doctor's approval, began treating Patrick bio-medically with supplements, vitamins, minerals, B-12 shots and other homeopathic therapies. He was almost six before he was potty-trained. And even that didn't happen until his mom had him treated in a hyperbaric oxygen chamber. Through her research, she found that autistic children couldn't feel like everyone else. So Patrick never felt the pressure of having to go to the bathroom until his many trips in the chamber brought that awareness to his senses. The combination of treatments and therapies has netted remarkable, long-lasting results. Six years later, Kim is proud to say that she has never had him on any prescription behavior disorder medicine.

"At this point, we're in a great place," says Kim proudly. "We've worked hard for six years and Patrick is doing so well. He's in third grade (right on track for his age). He has a special education teacher but she doesn't have to spend a lot of time with him." Patrick's IEP (Individualized Education Plan) hasn't changed in several years. He's in class with other children and thriving. "We find ourselves in a blessed place. We don't really have to make Patrick's condition our number one daily priority any more. After six years of expensive, hard, backbreaking work, he is functioning well and is happy."

Backbreaking is a good word for the battle the Spencers have endured to get to this point. Patrick's temper tantrums and stronger-than-life will brought on parent and child battles that often left Kim and Sam bruised and exhausted. They remained partners in all this, and yes, they are still married. The lack of speech development was their first indication. Most children can say at least two consecutive words as a means of communication by age two. Then most can verbalize three words in succession by age three. Patrick could count and point out objects but he couldn't tell his mother he was hungry. He knew every word to *Finding Nemo* and he could draw cartoon characters better than most adults. He obsessed violently over things like a certain color shirt. Kim says there was that "year of the yellow shirt." He wouldn't get dressed unless it was the color that he had adopted as his favorite color that year. Taking away the gluten and casein (a protein found in dairy products) produced the most immediate and most dramatic results. It was a good start but only the beginning for the ambitious parents who wanted only the best for their special child.

A year or so later, the Spencers introduced a treatment called chelation. This is a method of pulling out the heavy minerals in Patrick's little body. By pulling out the metals through chelation, coupled with hyperbaric treatments, his body was well-oxygenated, free of harmful chemicals and able to repair cell damage. The chelation and the hyperbaric oxygen treatments returned his ability to feel, to hurt and to know the needs of his body.

Another avenue Kim pursued involved treatment of the condition biologically as well as neurologically. "Look for deficiencies and pathogens in the body that need to be treated," says Kim. "Their immune systems don't function like normal kids'. They never seem sick and they seldom get a fever. Their immune system is overactive. They get pathogens in their body and they can't tell you they're sick. They can't tell you their stomach hurts. They just act out behaviorally. You have to treat the pathogens that are there and know to test for them."

For a short period, Patrick started getting into trouble, started biting himself and had become very aggressive. After several tests and many sleepless nights, Kim and Dr. Ramos discovered he had a bacterial infection. The negative behavior, the screaming and avoidance turned out to be a clostridia infection. Once the infection was treated, the aggressive behavior stopped.

Patrick has been through many physical therapy programs, most of them parent-driven. He has participated in play therapy groups and Kim even took him to Florida to start a new behavioral therapy called Relationship Development integration. She says the program was impressive but hard to continue on a regular basis.

Throughout all this, the Spencers have had to manage dealing with this challenging child, a newborn baby and the financial struggles that all these treatments and therapies bring about. In just the first year, they had spent $24,000 out of pocket on Patrick's treatments. Insurance covered only the most basic health issues. After that, Kim's parents began helping them by sending them a substantial amount every month.

While it took almost three years for experts to diagnose Patrick and for Kim to accept his condition, "now I could spot an 8-month-old with autism from the other side of a Walmart store," says Kim.

Today, Patrick still exhibits some of those all-too-recognizable traits. He tells stories and makes noise all day long. He can't interact normally with other children and has no real friends, expect for his sister, Anna Brooke. He still takes the stairs one by one coming down. He is sensitive to sunlight and has a constant battle with yeast that affects his bowels and behavior. He practically lives on anti-fungal meds. Comprehension questions are difficult for him. He can't, and probably won't, ever participate in team sports.

There are many achievements and lots of milestones to celebrate, however. His mom happily reports that he functions well in his third grade class with minimal support. He makes his grades, is very smart and keeps up. He is a sweet child who is truly remorseful when he gets in trouble. He's constantly creating things (even if it is out of trash, which drives his mom crazy). He "kicks butt" at Wii bowling, loves to swim and his teachers think he has a calling in children's theater. But the underlying condition still torments Kim and other advocates who have learned to adapt the hard way.

So what does this veteran of special needs recommend to other parents concerned their child might have a behavioral disorder?

1.  The sooner the parents start looking at options the better. Younger kids get better results faster. The sooner you see results, the more aggressively you will seek treatment.
2.  Find a DAN doctor (Defeat Autism Now—a network of doctors trained specifically in autism cases) or a pediatrician who is understanding and willing to work with you as you pursue the many courses of action.
3.  Read extensively about bio-medical treatments (autism is not just a mental disorder, contrary to how it is classified even now). Treat your child's behavior as a possible physical disorder. Hopefully, one day, the diagnosis will be reclassified and maybe patients can get better coverage from the insurance companies.
4.  Enroll the child in speech therapy, occupational therapy and physical therapy. These are crucial to the body's ability to operate. Explore other therapies as well—ABA therapy, DIR Floortime, even some therapeutic listening. All kids are different and all *autistic*

kids are different too. What works for one child, may not work for another. Most importantly, it may not work for the family. Find a therapy that works, and a therapist who is willing to try new things. Keep your child *engaged*!

5. Treat food as a medicine. Explore and experiment with food allergies and sensitivities.

Now that Patrick's condition is under control and his diagnosis has been upgraded to "highly functioning on the cusp of Aspberger's on the autism spectrum," Kim has found a vocation. The former broadcast journalist now serves as a patient advocate in her doctor's office. She is also a very vocal voice for the autism community, promoting research to find a cause and cure of this highly controversial condition. She's quick to point out to parents there's no cookie-cutter approach to autism. "Every child is different, every path a parent takes is different," she warns. "I wouldn't be able to just help Patrick. It's in my nature to share what I know to try to prevent this. I not only help parents whose children are affected but I mostly want to see that it doesn't happen at all. The numbers are growing and that breaks my heart. That's what my advocacy work is all about. What I really want is to no longer have a job." Kim's employer and Patrick's pediatrician, Dr. Ramon Ramos, is proud of Kim's work, "Since Kim joined my practice, I have been able to learn more about the diagnosis, care and the differences between all autistic children. Without her," Dr. Ramos says, "my autistic patients would not have progressed to the levels they have. Kim brings a tremendous support not only to my practice but to the children and their families."

While the cause of autism has never been determined definitely, there is an ever-growing and very vocal group that believes its cause is genetic but triggered by environmental factors.

Six years later, the autism advocate is still first and foremost a mom. It's hard to believe that she made a job out of finding information for her son, but she has done it and done it well. She revels in the antics of her now six and nine year old children. Anna Brooke is just now learning that her brother is "different." To her he's always been the same loving, irritating, funny, loud sibling that he has always been. "They're very typical. They fight and she mothers him. He irritates her and they get on each other's nerves," says Kim. When Anna Brooke first asked her mother about autism, Kim told her that Patrick was sick when he was little and that he just has to learn differently: "I tell her it's no big deal. We still love him." That's Patrick's success today. "This is what I was asking for when I prayed for children. I look at the two of them and I say 'bring it on!' It warms my heart to see that she loves him, and they do have a very typical brother/sister relationship. We are a strong family and we plan to stay that way."

## TWO YEARS LATER

The Spencers are now leading as close to a normal life as they ever thought possible. Patrick has made miraculous strides from being treated for the underlying medical issues that came along with his autism. He is now mainstreamed in 7th grade and is in the process of being reevaluated to determine whether he is still on the autism spectrum. Mom and Dad could not be more proud of his progress and accomplishments. Kim also jumped into the literary arena-as a contributor in the recently released book, *Thinking Mom's Revolution*. The book is now in it's second printing and has sparked an online revolution on a blog (www.thinkingmomsrevolution.com) and on Facebook.

# Hugh Markowsky

### More Than Just an Itch

He'd always had challenges with severe eczema. Around the end of second grade, his classmates were preparing for First Communion. But Hugh Markowsky was struggling with some inflamed spots on his forehead.

This beginning of his journey might have seemed simple enough. The doctors who were treating him tried everything to minimize his discomfort and to get the eczema under control. Another lesion on his back that his mother, Genevieve, thought was a spider bite had been an ongoing enigma to the medical community and his family. The longer they waited, the worse the condition became. Hugh was repeatedly and exhaustingly tested but his high eosinophil count (white blood cells that become active when you have certain allergic diseases, infections, and other medical conditions) threw the doctors off track from the real culprit. His immune system was compromised, the eczema was excruciating, his skin was peeling, and he felt like his body was on fire.

After culturing that lesion, doctors diagnosed Hugh with MRSA (Methicillin-Resistant Staphylococcus Aureus), a potentially deadly staff infection that defies traditional treatments.

His mother was terrified and relieved at the same time. "Looking back, I know I was in shock and extremely depressed. The care was so intense and caused so him much pain. Nobody was giving us any definitive answer. All they would tell us is 'it's gonna take a long time.' They said it could be allergies. We started investigating for ourselves," Genevieve recalls. "I think the reason the MRSA got out of control is because it went undiagnosed for so long and when it took hold, he was too weak. It had gotten into his blood stream. It doesn't usually get as bad as his had gotten. But we'd see the symptoms, put him on antibiotics and wait for results of the test. Testing for MRSA is inadequate and it came back negative time after time."

Throughout the two-year span while Hugh was getting weaker and weaker, his family was doing all they could to keep the MRSA from returning. Genevieve battled to keep house sterile and germ free and family members were tested. The immediate family all took antibiotics to keep it from progressing to other members. It is even recommended that family pets are cultured since they can possibly pass it from pet to human. When doctors prescribed steroids for him, it cleared up his scaly lesions but they suppressed his immune system. "Every time he would go on steroids to get his skin clear, the MRSA would flare back up because his immune system was suppressed," remembers the frustrated Genevieve.

"He was waking up screaming in pain every few hours at night. We didn't sleep more than a few hours a night for 18 months and I was trying to work full time. I was sleep-deprived and depressed. I'd go to the physician's offices. I was disheveled, exhausted, and I know they looked at me like I was a typical hysterical mother. I was on the brink of a breakdown. And Hugh was dying."

Hugh's organs were so toxic from the MRSA, the family made a rushed trip to the Augusta Burn Center. His organs were shutting down from all the MRSA invading his body. The symptoms mimicked Stevens-Johnson's Syndrome (a rare, serious disorder in which your skin and mucous membranes react severely to a medication or infection. Often, Stevens-Johnson syndrome begins with flu-like symptoms, followed by a painful red or purplish rash that spreads and blisters, eventually causing the top layer of your skin to die and shed). At the Burn Center, the doctors ran skin biopsies and a series of tests that red flagged the seriousness of his depleted immune system. Unfortunately, too much attention was focused on the eczema and allergies instead of the now-apparent condition of his immune system. The normal levels for a healthy person taking the allergy test are 250. Hugh's numbers were into the thousands. Three more agonizing hospital stays later, the answer arrived.

By an act of God or a simple fluke, the family learned about a doctor in Atlanta who ultimately saved Hugh's life. But Hugh was too sick to fly and he needed to get there STAT. While at Memorial, a physical therapist told the family about Angel Flight (a non-profit group that arranges free air transportation for charitable and medical needs). In his condition, he would never be able to fly on a traditional airline. With a doctor's note, this privately funded service will transport patients free of charge. Hugh was put on the plane. Two hours later, Dr. K. Balcarek of Sandy Springs Pediatrics took one look at Hugh and recognized the symptoms instantly. It was Halloween and Genevieve knew that her beautiful boy was going to die if someone didn't figure out how to treat him. He was in excruciating pain, his skin was falling off his body, the scabs were oozing and his body was red hot to the touch. They knew they had to act fast. Hugh was no longer able to walk and was lethargic and barely able to speak. Dr. Balcarek prescribed morphine for the pain, and ran a series of tests. Hugh was put on a cocktail of antibiotics, increased fluids and a regimen of IVIg treatments (IVIg is a plasma product formed by taking antibodies from about 20,000 donors and mixing them together). The combination of antibiotics and IVIg to revive his immune system brought about the miraculous improvement Genevieve had been waiting two years to happen. "It was a miracle he was still alive and the MRSA wasn't in his organs and bones—truly a miracle," says Genevieve. It was also a miracle that he didn't have to have surgery. Some kids with his advanced stage of

MRSA have terrible scars on their heart and he had none of that. It was definitely prayers that got him through those horrible three years.

"It was such a test of faith. I can't make sense out of why everything went wrong for so long. We had all the resources anyone could have to fight this (including a very respected physician who is Hugh's grandfather). We just needed someone to figure out what was causing this. It was like going through the desert for forty years, when the answer is ten miles away."

Even at his sickest moments, Hugh seldom complained. He didn't like needles and fought like a tiger until they finally had to anesthetize him to "stick" him.

Remembering Hugh's response to even that first IVIg transfusion, Genevieve says it was astonishing. In only two days, he literally jumped out of his wheelchair and started playing with toys and being funny. "I thought, 'Oh my God, my son is back!' He had that dramatic a response to the IVIg." That was the beginning of an eight-month regimen. Hugh improved month-by-month, day-by-day. "After the first six months, I felt like he was animated, active, engaged—the old Hugh," recalls Genevieve. "My only concern was that, after he was through with the IVIg treatments, would his immune system stay strong or would he face a lifetime of infusions? That was the unknown and my greatest concern at that point in his recovery."

Her fears have proven unfounded and after two years out of school, Hugh returned to his friends and the classrooms at Blessed Sacrament School in Savannah. "Seeing him with friends, being able to touch him and know he's not hurting, looking at smooth normal skin, it still overwhelms me. Hugh will say, 'Remember I'd wake up and take my pajamas off and then my skin would come off? Gosh that was awful.' Then he'd run out and play. Kids are so resilient and amazing."

Genevieve credits her strong family support system with her own resiliency. Her mother, father, sister and niece were always there for her and for Hugh. "I can't imagine how I could have done this (without them). I don't know how single mothers with sick children do it. It was such a relief to have the emotional support and just having someone there. It helped to have someone say 'you're not crazy, this is happening.' They kept telling me we're gonna figure this out."

Two years have passed since the momentous meeting with Dr. Balcarek and Genevieve never takes Hugh's health for granted. "I feel confident that we have knocked out the MRSA for good. But, if by some fluke, he contracts it again, at least I'll know what to do and where to go. That's like anyone coming out of a war zone and ending up in a beautiful nation. You never really trust that everything is going to be all right. But now knowing what to do if it ever happens again, that's the biggest relief."

## TWO YEARS LATER

Hugh continues to thrive and improve. He will graduate soon from 8th grade and move on to high school. He is a happy, healthy young man who is a joy to the family. He is currently MRSA free and his family thanks God every day and prays for continued good health!

# Birney Bull

## *THE* Adoption Attorney and Special Father

Birney Bull is a man with a passion. He's a pro-life advocate who lives his conviction. While he could have chosen a more profitable legal specialty, Birney chose adoptions as his forté and has helped more than 300 families find children and children find parents.

During his career he has also placed a good number of special needs children into loving homes. He's excellent at what he does not just because of his legal expertise but also because he's the dad of Amy, a Down syndrome child who has overcome enormous health issues. Birney borrowed a thought from Mother Theresa, "God doesn't give you more than you can handle. I sometimes wonder why he thinks I can handle so MUCH!"

Because he and his wife, Deborah, *can*.

The couple first suspected there was a problem during genetic testing. Deborah was 41 and the Down syndrome diagnosis came out early on. Birney and Deborah were also informed about severe cardiac problems at that time. Amy, like some Down syndrome children, had a hole in her heart. But she also had another, more rare condition—the right side of her heart was smaller than her left. At the time of her birth, doctors felt if they rebuilt that wall, her right side wouldn't be able to keep up. The doctors proposed letting Amy live with a two-chamber heart indefinitely. But when she was five, the right side of the heart had grown substantially and they decided to close the wall. She was in cardiac ICU for days after this corrective open-heart surgery. Things weren't going well. "The cardiologist kept mentioning 'Plan B' if she didn't respond to this procedure," remembers Birney. "For 48 hours she could survive with fluids pumping in to the right side of her heart to keep it functioning. But time was running out and the doctors didn't know what they'd do next. At 46 hours, she started responding." Her blood oxygen saturation was also a concern. The normal numbers are from 98 to 100. Her normal rate was in the low 80s for the first five years of her life. As she got closer and closer to the surgery, she was in the 70s. "For us," Bernie says, "if we got to 93, we'd be calling 9-1-1. Her system would compensate. She even pulled a 60 one time during complications after her second surgery. Now she hovers around 92, but that's so much better than it used to be."

Now at ten, Amy is thriving. She is articulate and verbal but her words aren't always clear. She's in third grade at Marshpoint Elementary, where she recently played Sally Ride, the first woman astronaut in a school play. She couldn't memorize her lines like others in the class, but she got around that with a creative PowerPoint presentation.

So when Attorney Birney Bull tells a family he knows about special needs adoption, he means it. "Legally, it's exactly the same process except that adoption law is complicated and technical. It's gotten more and more regulated," says Birney. The Interstate Compact addresses adoptions across state lines. It is a treaty among the states to arrange and approve the home study and assure a healthy home for the child. Parents wanting to adopt a special needs child will be scrutinized more closely to make sure the parents know what they're getting into. Whether it's a special needs case or an international adoption, Birney knows there are issues facing the parents. "There are identity issues in adopting a child. When you get up and see across your breakfast table someone with features like your own, it grounds you," he says. "The adopted child doesn't have that. Many times parents know what they're getting. With a special needs adoption, most parents are prepared but there are some who find out after the adoption's taken place. If you adopt an infant with autism, the diagnosis doesn't usually occur until age three.

"But what I've found is that parents of special needs kids get to see things other parents never get to see. You see the world through your kid's eyes. You see the world differently when you have a child with a disability."

Birney says it takes a special person to adopt a special needs child, "I call that emotional elasticity. Some people just want to be parents. But the people who are willing to take on a child with special needs, can adapt more readily and easily to the challenges of raising one of these children than average parents can."

"I wish people could know that being around a special needs child or people with disabilities shows you what matters. It matters that you share with those people. This person may have a mobility or cognitive problem. Being able to walk or solve problems are nice things. But that's not humanity. Humanity is the spark that jumps between two people and makes them care about each other. And that connects them to God. I think learning THAT is a heck of a lot more important than saying someone happens to have Down syndrome. I wish people could recognize the benefit of being around people with special needs and what they can teach us. It's not your IQ and not your income that's important, but your ability to love. *That* is who you are."

## TWO YEARS LATER

Amy is doing well as a 6th grader at Coastal Middle School. Her older sister, Betsy, is a senior at the Savannah College of Art and Design, and also has numerous interests. She does a lot of tutoring (mostly math, but some science and English too, as well as SAT prep). She also works in an alterations shop on Wilmington Island, among other things. Deborah is in her 27th year of teaching Fibers at SCAD. Birney still does "the adoption thing."

# From Foster Care to Adoption
## The Branch Family

For Josette and Robert Branch, having other people's children in their care is nothing new. Since becoming foster parents seven years ago, they have taken in a 17-year-old boy, a 16 year-old-girl, three children from one family (aged two to four), and another little boy for almost three years. All of these children were loved, cared for and returned to their parents after varying time spans in the Branch home.

But nine-year-old Jaydah didn't go back to her biological home. She was adopted by the Branches at age six after living with them a year. Next, two-year-old Robert III came into their home and was soon legally and permanently adopted. Robert III is now four and has come a long way!

Robert first came to stay as a foster child with the Branch family when he was barely over a year old. He has Cerebral Palsy. He couldn't walk or crawl. He couldn't communicate. His left arm was barely functioning. Before the year was out, the Branches were asked if they'd like to adopt him, and the answer was a resounding "yes!"

"When we first got him, he would cry because he didn't want to walk. He just wanted to scoot across the floor," says Josette. "But we walked him all over the house holding him up with his hands. We had to make him use his legs to get them stronger and you should see him now!"

Robert's still developmentally about a year behind other four-year-olds but what a difference the Branch family has made with him. He knows his colors and shapes but hasn't learned to write or recognize any sight words. He is still in speech therapy to correct a speech impediment and his left arm is still weaker than the right. To look at him, one would never guess that he has a disability. Josette says people often tell the little bespectacled child that he looks like Arthur from the cartoon that comes on Public Television. "If I could go back to Atlanta (where the Branches lived when they adopted Jaydah and Robert) I know those case workers who saw the way he was before would be so surprised. When I say he's now a typical kid, I mean he's a rough, happy little boy."

The older Branch children, Brian Butler (24) and Marya (17) were skeptical at first with the additions to their family. Marya had been the only one left in the house when the little ones started arriving. But now? "She loves them to death," says Josette proudly. "They may fuss a little but she and Brian love them so much."

The challenges of taking in a child with Cerebral Palsy weren't just about mobility. Robert had trouble eating. There were certain foods he couldn't tolerate because his palate was so deep. Some food had to be ground up in order for him to swallow or it would get stuck at the roof of his mouth. Potty training was a challenge but he's finally mastered it and Josette couldn't be more proud of him. "You have to be able to treat a child as if they were your own. You just love them, stay patient and be understanding. You have to be compassionate. You work hard to do whatever it takes to makes sure that child is safe because he has already been through so much."

At a court hearing Josette ran into Robert's mother who thanked her for all she had done for her child. The mother explained that she wasn't able to take care of him but was grateful that he had found such a good home.

Josette knows that her children will not stay small forever, and she has the same dreams for Robert that she does for her older children. "I want him to grow up and be independent. I want him to be able to take care of himself and have a family." Josette was encouraged to meet a 70-something year old man with CP who had lived the life she wants for Brian. The gentleman had married, had children of his own, and enjoyed a successful career. His bit of advice to her was to continue the speech therapy. That was something that wasn't available when he was growing up.

"I treat Jaydah and Robert like they were my own," says Josette. "My husband and I just love them and do everything we can to make sure they're taken care of so they'll grow up and be independent. You just love them, love them, love them. Robert never gets enough kisses from me!"

## TWO YEARS LATER

Josette's brood continues to thrive. Jaydah is in the 6th grade now and is on High Honor Roll. She is 12 years old and is "doing wonderfully," says the proud Josette. Robert is in the 1st grade and is improving nicely. He talks nonstop and has plenty of energy. "It's hard for me to keep up with him." He still goes to physical therapy, occupational therapy and speech therapy weekly. "I can't believe he is 6 years old now. Both children are a joy to have in our lives. They have really been a blessing to me and my husband. We are thankful every day."

# Their Child has DIFFERENT ABILITIES
## The Hussey Family

When Pam and Brian Hussey realized that Mother Nature had a later-in-life gift for them, they were thrilled and a bit apprehensive. Their children, Ryan and Brennan, were 21 and 15 when their baby brother, Sean, entered their world. "We were obviously shocked," laughs Brian. "But God apparently decided we were gonna have another child. I looked at Pam and said, 'well, the only thing we've done *really* well in our lives is raise children. And I guess we're going to do it again.'"

This staunchly Christian couple wasn't interested in prenatal testing, "not even a little bit," says Brian. Even though Pam was in the age group where testing is encouraged, they politely declined. "Why would we? What was the purpose? We wouldn't do anything different even if we did find out something," says Brian. "The only thing we wanted to know was whether or not we were having a boy or girl so we'd know what color to paint the nursery."

But, on that exciting day when Pam's C-section was scheduled, there was a lot to discover. Their obstetrician pulled Brian aside after only a quick look at the newborn and warned that Sean may have Down syndrome. Brian didn't believe what she was saying, "I asked, 'what makes you think that?'" She told him the baby has short fingers and low muscle tone in his chest. "I said I'd never seen a baby that didn't have low muscle tone," argued Brian. She told the now distraught father that Sean had Asian-like features. Again, Brian didn't believe it, but decided against telling Pam until she had rested. By the time she had slept and began recovering from her surgery, they talked and realized that Sean, in fact, had Down syndrome.

"I admit that at first, it was hard," recalls Brian. "I was happy Sean was healthy and Pam was okay. It was difficult until we started coming to terms with it. The social workers at the hospital made copies of information about Down syndrome and gave them to Pam. They tried to be as comforting and informative as possible but they were not very knowledgeable. We were on our own to find out more." The Husseys were thrilled to learn that, "thankfully," Sean had none of the serious health issues that some children with Down syndrome have. "We were told, 'yes he's fine.' You can take him home and raise him like other children. We relied on the internet to get as much information as we could."

Soon, the Husseys would find more support. When Sean was about three months old, the family was introduced to Babies Can't Wait. BCW staff started coming to their home and working with Sean. At six months, the enthusiastic parents began using sign language to communicate with Sean. It took a few months before they realized that Sean was not only understanding the signs but was able to start reproducing them himself. "At about 10 months old, Sean responded to one of his first signs. He saw a watermelon and he signed 'ball.'" said Brian. "It was the first time he signed to us. He saw a round object, thought it was a ball and made us realize he was getting it!" Sean is now five years old and still isn't talking much. But he can communicate many of his thoughts and needs through sign language. Unfortunately, Brian wasn't with Sean when he made his first sign, but Pam called Brian immediately from the grocery store to share the exciting news.

Sean's successful development didn't happen overnight and it wasn't because of luck. A lot of hard work and parental dedication have brought Sean to the place he is today. Sean has benefitted from many private physical and occupational therapy sessions to work on his major motor skills and fine motor skills as well. He is involved in the Babies Can Read programs. Family members read to him daily and are proud that he comprehends on a second grade level. Sean has started verbalizing words and some sentences. "We make him ask for things," says Brian. "When he used to sign for a Popsicle, we would get it for him. Now, he has to say 'May I please have a Popsicle (red or blue).' It's still very remedial but he is verbalizing and we're thrilled."

Brian's worried at times that sign language would become a crutch because he's so good at it. He's up to 700 signs. "We're doing everything we can to challenge Sean's cognitive skills," says Brian. "I think we've done all the right things. I'm okay with Sean's expressive delay. If he understands what's going on around him and has ability to learn yet is delayed in expressing what he's learning, I'm okay with that. Eventually the day will come when Sean will be talking so much we'll wish for the days when he couldn't talk. I much prefer Sean's delays to be expressive. I'd rather him be able to understand and not express than express and not understand. I'd rather him read at a second grade level and not be able to speak as well. Those skills will come. His cognitive skills and his ability to learn are much more rewarding than his ability to talk."

*Brian*'s ability to talk and also to make things happen have been crucial in the continuing development of a growing and prosperous non-profit for families of Down syndrome children. It's called Lowcountry Down Syndrome Society and it was founded by John and Candy Bogardis five years ago. Just like Sean has inspired Brian and Pam, the Bogardis' daughter, Lainey, sparked a need in them to help others. In just the past few years, the LDSS-sponsored Buddy Walk has grown to 3,500 participants. The organization is in its third year sponsoring Camp Buddy, which provides a bridge for these children from one school year to the next. The group puts on the annual Night of Champions, which is a lavish banquet to recognize adults with developmental disabilities who are actively working and thriving in this community. Employers who hire these special citizens are also recognized for "looking past the label and giving them the opportunity," says Brian. "Our goal is to have more businesses in the community recognize the benefits of having people with different abilities in their employment." LDSS was also chosen as an official charity partner of the Rock and Roll Savannah Marathon. "It's gonna be huge!" says Brian, the current president of the Lowcountry Down Syndrome Society.

In his role as president, Brian has become not just the head volunteer administrator, but he's clearly the head cheerleader for LDSS, for children with different abilities and, of course, for Sean. "Brian is such an attentive dad. He wants [Sean] to be a typical kid," says LDSS co-founder Candy Bogardis. "He wants all our kids to lead the lives God put them here for. Brian believes we can change the way society looks at our children and see them as the contributors they can be. He is a huge advocate, whether it's for change in the schools or sports, he wants Sean and the rest of these children to have the same opportunities."

"It's obvious that Sean can't climb or walk steps or do things other five year olds can do," says Brian. "But I'm amazed at Sean's ability to learn and his joy for life. It's what we always try to stress to people. Children with all types of different abilities are children first. The sooner we get that, the better we all are. They are children. They run, they laugh, they play. They do everything other children do. They just do it differently.

"And in fifteen years when Sean is 20, he is going to be much better prepared to be productive in our community. Twenty-five years ago, parents weren't challenging their children in the same ways we are today. My job (as LDSS president and Sean's dad) is to prepare society to look past the obvious. Instead of just being the grocery bagger, maybe our children can be the assistant produce manager or assistant manger. Can't an adult with developmental disabilities be a bookkeeper? Can we look past the current labels and change the way we think?"

Brian says that's what Sean has done for him. "I constantly have to challenge myself and ask, 'what is my vision for Sean?' Well, I think that's our job not only as parents but as a community."

"Not that many years ago, having a special needs child had a negative stigma in the community and family," says Candy. "Parents thought they were a burden and the community didn't help. These children are not and never have been a burden. Community awareness has come a long way. In our generation we can now see people's differences as a positive."

"Sean has opened our eyes. I knew very little about people with different abilities. This has given us an opportunity to understand and have an impact in not just Sean's life, but our community around us. I think we (LDSS) are having an impact in our community. From my few speaking engagements and getting around town, I have more and more people come to me and say, 'I've heard of what you all are doing. I think it's wonderful.'"

# TWO YEARS LATER . . .

Sean Hussey has been in school and is loving it. His last three years have been in a true inclusion environment in Savannah. While he has his obvious limitations, he has done very well in the academic environment—scholastically and socially. His cognitive development still seems to be on pace with children his age. His expressive development continues to be delayed-he doesn't talk a lot but is reading at grade level ahead of his class. He will read to his parents and they know what he is saying. Sean loves his school, loves his friends and enjoys the work. "There is no question the early intervention of teaching him sign language benefitted Sean," says his proud dad. "It helped his cognitive and social development. It reduced some of the frustration of not being able to communicate." Sean is horseback riding, bowling with the AMBUCS, taking karate and is "so busy." He still continues his therapies outside of school. "Sean's peers don't see him as being different," said Brian. "They know he has differences but it is inspiring to see how they treat him. He may not be the first picked in a game of kickball, but they want him to play with them. A lot of times this is without encouragement from adults. Kids don't see him as different. He's a normal happy kid—just with a few differences."

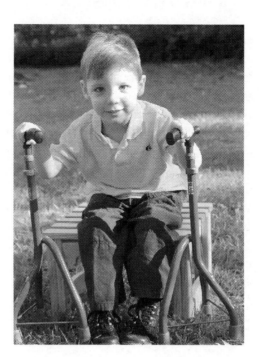

# Stephen's Story
### Learning to Walk

Eva Elmer learned that her child, Stephen, had been diagnosed with Cerebral Palsy before leaving the hospital after his birth. Several months later, she was told that he could possibly have to live out his life in a wheelchair. After several months of observation, it appeared that dire assessment could be correct. Eva had sadly begun to accept this devastating prognosis when, a few years later, she found the miracle she had been looking for.

Stephen McNeill Coleman was born in 2008 after a difficult pregnancy. At 23 weeks, Eva's placenta ruptured and she was hospitalized for four-and-a-half weeks. Eva was bedridden, trying to stave off delivery of Stephen and his twin for as long as possible. When the babies had reached almost 29 gestational weeks, an infection set in and the doctors decided to take them by emergency Caesarean Section. Stephen was tiny and needed another seven weeks in the hospital before he could come home. His twin sister didn't survive, passing away twelve hours after her birth because her lungs weren't developed enough to survive.

When Stephen was in the NICU (Neonatal Intensive Care Unit), Eva learned that he had suffered from a lack of oxygen sometime during delivery or in utero. This is all-too-common when the amniotic fluid is infected, causing trauma to the unborn child. The longer the child is deprived of oxygen, the more involved the Cerebral Palsy—and the more severe the consequences. A few weeks after he was born, doctors ordered an MRI that confirmed

Periventricular Leukomalacia (brain damage). It manifested itself as Spastic Diplegia Cerebral Palsy (affecting his legs). But Eva was told she wouldn't know the extent of the damage until Stephen started missing milestones.

As the beautiful, smiling baby got older, the signs were obvious and the milestones were, in fact, being missed. He maintained the stiff, rigid posture of a typical CP baby. He missed rolling over. Crawling wasn't even a remote possibility. He couldn't grasp objects with his hands.

But Eva wasn't giving up. She started Stephen on occupational therapy at five months, then added physical therapy. Much later, she added speech therapy to his weekly routine.

A few months shy of his second birthday, Eva had become discouraged by Stephen's lack of progress despite his rigid regimen of therapies and the hard work of the professional and caring therapists who couldn't seem to break through to the unyielding child. She began researching websites for a summer camp for children with Cerebral Palsy and/or conditions similar to Stephen's. That's when she found out about the Grace Center in Bluffton, South Carolina, and a progressive therapy program called Conductive Education. At the time, there was no room for Stephen at the camp. She later learned that the center had closed but the directors, Peter and Erica Bartos, were still operating out of their home. It wasn't long before Eva got her acceptance letter. They had room for Stephen!

Eva and Stephen began the commute to Bluffton (50 minutes from their home in Savannah) five days a week for twelve hours per week. The CE (Conductive Education) approach focuses on training the brain to learn proper movements. For a child that can't walk, it means figuring out how to take steps without any ambulatory devices other than therapeutic shoes. CE conductors (as their therapists are called) tell parents that if the brain is forced, it will figure out a way to connect the mind with muscle. In typical humans without this condition, the mind and the muscle interact thoughtlessly. For a CP patient, it takes tremendous effort for the brain to figure out how to make the leg walk or the arm to lift or the head to stay up. Before Stephen started this aggressive approach, he was unable to stand for very long, couldn't take steps, and couldn't even hold onto a squishy ball. After three weeks, he was able to grasp a push toy and take steps with some help for balance. This technique teaches the child to make the movements while strengthening the body and learning flexibility. It's a repetitive process, taught with patience and gentle diligence. The results have been nothing short of "miraculous," says the proud mom.

After just twelve weeks in the program, Stephen can now grasp and hold objects. He can pick things up and place them in a basket. He can now pull himself along the floor, which he had never done before. He pulls off his socks and can now walk pushing the walker for short distances that get longer every week. In addition to these motor skills, he also has academic lessons. Stephen is working on his ABCs, colors, animals and loves to work on puzzles. Conductive Education is a holistic approach of training the mind and the body. Almost to the day Stephen started walking, he also began talking and became visibly more aware of his surroundings.

"My dream is for him to enter a regular school," says Eva. "I want him to be independently mobile and I truly believe it's possible if we continue this program."

This summer, Stephen will stay in Orlando for the CE summer camp, going through an intensive four-week program. Then he'll be back to his daily routine of travel to Bluffton for more of the two-hour therapy sessions. It's not an easy commitment, but it's one that has proven results for her only child. "I was desperate and so depressed (before CE)," says Eva. "I was so sad that he wasn't getting better."

Sometimes the staff will spend as much as 30 minutes waiting for Stephen to crawl across the floor. They don't give up and they don't help him. They wait until he is gently coaxed and motivated to make the move on his own. Stephen's neurologist now predicts Stephen will walk by age three or, at the latest, four. "They can wait 30-35 minutes and all he crawls is maybe five feet. But he's got to do it himself," says Eva. "He loves going there. And he's so happy with himself and his accomplishments. He's got more confidence and he loves to walk. It's a miracle."

## TWO YEARS LATER

Stephen has been working hard on his skills but his spasticity was catching up to him as he reached four-five years old. Botox injections and exercise couldn't keep those muscles from tightening and he was losing function and heading to a wheelchair full time. He underwent a selective dorsal rhizotomy (SDR) in July 2013 which takes out all spasticity in the body and now he has a second chance with his "new legs" to get back on his way to gaining function and reaching his full potential.

# Sarena James—Superblogger

## Onaisle9.com

Sweet, joyful, faith-filled, loving—those are just a few of the adjectives to describe Sarena James, one Rockin' Autism MOM!

Already a blessed mother of (now 11-year-old) daughter Jaydn, Serena and her television news anchor husband, Raphael, felt their cup was overflowing when they learned their second child was a boy. Grant (now 5) was soon followed by baby sister, Nia. The James household was full and busy!

Sarena's pregnancies were uneventful. Each birth was greeted with the same amount of joy and thanksgiving. The first 18 months of Grant's life were completely normal until, at around two, he stopped talking. "Autism had never been a word in our vocabulary," said Sarena. "But his behavior changed—the absence of speech, his running back and forth, flicking the lights on and off and the vacant stares. We started a series of assessments and found it was autism.

"I remember that day in that office. I wondered, how can I breathe? The air had gone out of the room. I remember we went to the car and wondered 'what does this mean?' I decided the question from that day forward was 'can he learn?' And if the answer is yes, we have to figure out how to make that happen." At the time he wouldn't look at his parents. There was no eye contact or language for a whole year. Sarena was worried she had gotten her answer and it wasn't the one she wanted.

It was confusing for the busy mother because physically, Grant was perfect. They took it slow, asking him questions, probing his actions and searching for the right place for their silent child.

She found an elementary school with all the tools necessary to deal with a child with Grant's challenges. It was tough putting that precious 3-year-old on a bus, hoping and praying that he would understand. The staff at his school was incredible. He started the class in a little Rifton chair (seat with constraints). Sarena sat outside the classroom and "cried her eyes out" hoping she'd done the right thing.

Fast forward two years and it was *clearly* the "right thing" for Grant. Sarena says last summer "the window of learning" his therapists had talked about "completely flew open." One morning, Sarena came downstairs and found Grant had spelled out "Grant James" on his own with magnetic letters. "We realized there is somebody in there!" said his exuberant mom. The family has a nine-foot chalkboard wall devoted to the kids and Grant is always busy writing on it. He writes the names of the stars and what grocery store he wants to visit. He now has over a hundred words and they are appropriate and he speaks—yes, *speaks* them—in context. While riding around looking at the lights, there was Grant's little voice from the back seat saying, "Move, cars, please!" The James family celebrates each and every milestone!

"Even if we have to use different roadmaps, Grant has answered the initial question, 'can you learn?'" said Sarena. "For any parent, that's what you want to know. And when the answer is 'yes,' you say, 'okay, buddy, let's do this thing.'"

This "thing" involved not just the education and therapy regimen for Grant, but it meant communication therapy for the entire family and ultimately, the autism community. Sarena and Raphael started a now-nationally renowned blog called onaisle9.com. It's an interactive, informational website for parents of special needs children.

Onaisle9.com got its name because it represents the frustration of the James family and all parents who've ever experienced an out-of-control child. And it also represents the need for a "judgment-free zone" which calls for outsiders to be compassionate and nonjudgmental. "Our son has no physical signs something could be wrong," says Sarena. "There's no wheelchair, no facial movements or abnormalities. When meltdowns come, people think it's behavioral. They think better parenting would take care of this screaming child. How do you say to somebody, 'Do you even know what autism is?'" A turning point in Sarena's life happened on aisle 9 in Target one day. "Grant was having a meltdown. I felt by myself. The atmosphere was already tense dealing with this tantrumming child. The last thing I needed was people looking at us and passing judgment on our child or me. I came home that day thinking no one understands."

That incident "on aisle 9" prompted Sarena to write an article, *Judgment-Free Zone.* She sent it to Renee Seiler of www.goodenoughmother.com. To Sarena's amazement, Seiler included the article on her website. Sarena was blown away by the number of people who commented on her article and the knowledge that so many other parents were struggling with the same feelings and concerns. Sarena knew she was not alone and she and Raphael decided to create their own outlet for communication and idea sharing.

When the dynamic duo (Sarena and Raphael) started onaisle9, people began sharing similar stories and similar concerns. "It is my goal to challenge people to look at things from a different perspective," says the very optimistic Sarena. "I encourage them to use perspective, understanding and sensitivity. You wouldn't believe the emails we have gotten. Someone wrote: 'I was around a screaming child today. What I did was try not to add to that tense atmosphere. Instead I asked if there was something I could do to help.' That's what we're praying for. Instead of people mumbling or giving our family dirty looks, they can ask themselves what they can do to keep from bringing down the atmosphere. They can help by not adding to what the family has to deal with."

For the families of special needs children, the site is informational and therapeutic. "The more you talk, the more you learn and grow as you learn about others' journeys. The families learn as I did that there are so many people out there—that you're not alone," says Sarena. "Parents are willing to meet "on aisle 9," participate in the conversations, share experiences, they find that we can better the lives of our children. And don't we owe them that?"

Sarena and the frequent visitors to onaisle9.com come to the site for information—whether they have a special needs child or know a challenging child. Everybody who visits learns and shares from his or her perspective. New parents are treated with honesty and respect. In the blog, they are able to talk about their pain and fears. But Sarena is proud that throughout onaisle9. com, families can always find hope in the midst of darkness. In her own family, writing has helped them stay balanced. "My mother wrote an article called "From a Grandmother's Heart." In our minds, it was always *our son* that had autism. We never thought about how my mother felt having a grandson with these special needs. Three years later I now know how she feels. I said, 'Oh my God, it's affected you too!' My 11-year-old daughter came home a few weeks ago with an assignment to write a six-word memoir. It said, "Cute, Baby, Disorder, Still My Brother." I boo-hooed. We always felt she would talk about it when she was ready in her way. The sisters, Jaydn and Nia, now have to deal with Grant too. We believe that God not only thought out how the parents would relate to this child, He has also thought out how the siblings are going to live with him. They are amazing with Grant. Stern when they need to be, but patient."

Grant is still "moderately autistic but he is learning!" says the proud mother. He is being mainstreamed in one class. It is a challenge for him to sit still and not have one-on-one attention. And there are other challenges but for a child who said nothing and now can write his name and can identify his family, he has come a long way. His language is being used appropriately and for that, the James family rejoices. "Inches add up and eventually become miles! I am so grateful that he's *in there!* For a long time, he would just take my hand and point to things he wanted. Now he's naming them!"

And if other parents benefit from their website, that's cause for celebration as well. But the real victory comes when non-special needs individuals learn to reserve judgment. "With our son, there's nothing to clue you in that he is autistic. We may know he's screaming because something is too loud or lights are bothering him or because he's searching for a word, but others may not. We call on people to enter a *judgment-free zone*. When people do that, we know we are enlightening those around us while we continue on this journey." And when they see progress in Grant or in the surrounding community, the James family celebrates!

## TWO YEARS LATER

Grant James continues to make great strides including more language skills and even following multiple-step directives. "This journey has not been an easy one to travel," admits his mother, Serena. "There have been many potholes of tantrums and unexpected detours of learning styles, and even traffic jams of words trying to find the best route out. The scenery is ever-changing, along with the behavior. But we have learned to stop and celebrate the smallest of victories, because they do add up."

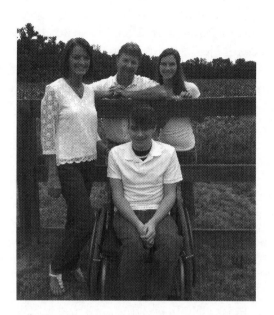

# Jeremy Patterson
## Somebody's Always Got it Worse

Angie Patterson will tell you in a heartbeat that she has a wonderful life. She has two beautiful children, a loving husband. She is blessed. And that blessing includes a son, Jeremy, born with Spina Bifida.

The soft-spoken, easy-going mother has a simple philosophy that keeps her happy and her family content. She focuses on what the Pattersons can do, not what they can't.

It took several years for Angie to get to this peaceful place in her life. Her daughter, Lindsay, was not yet two years old when Angie's AFP test (Alpha Fetal Protein) came back suspicious. Then two subsequent sonograms revealed an abnormal shape to Jeremy's head. The amniocentesis came back 99% positive that the baby in utero had Spina Bifida. Angie says knowing ahead of time helped the family and the doctors prepare.

The day Jeremy was born by Caesarean Section, he was wheeled out of the delivery room and into the operating room. He was born with a hole in his back with his spine outside his body. His spine was not completely closed and was encased along with many nerves in a sack outside his tiny infant body.

The less-than-24-hour-old baby underwent surgery to put the spine back inside his body and to close the deficit in his back. Unfortunately and unavoidably, nerves were damaged in this process. For Jeremy, it affected his ability to walk because he can't feel his legs. He also has bladder and bowel issues that resulted from repairing the spinal relocation.

A common side effect of Spina Bifida is hydrocephalus, which is excessive fluid around the brain. A week after he was born, Jeremy underwent his second surgery to implant a shunt that could drain the fluid. Unfortunately, the shunt became infected and had to be removed. A new one was put in after the infection cleared. The shunt proved to be problematic for the first five years of his life but is now manageable and is only noticeable when he when wears his hair short. "You can feel a lump and there are a couple of scars where other shunts have been removed," says Angie. "He doesn't care about the current scar showing. He looks better with short hair and doesn't care if people can see his scar."

Coming home from the hospital with a Spina Bifida child was frightening to the Pattersons. "All moms are nervous when you bring your baby home," says Angie. "But knowing that the shunt could malfunction keeps you on your toes. Every little cry or whine—all the things babies do—there was an added concern and made me so nervous."

Being told her son might never roll over and may never walk turned into a waiting game for the whole family. Doctors really didn't know what an SB child is capable of and their job is to prepare a family for the worst. Jeremy accomplished almost all his tasks, but in his own time. He did roll over and he crawled, "I cried like a baby when he crawled and I called everybody!" laughs Angie. She got her "best Christmas present ever" the year Jeremy walked on his crutches just days before the holiday. He accomplished this amazing feat after only a few sessions of his pre-school intervention class. Now that he's older and much bigger, walking isn't practical. Now he can stand on his crutches with his leg braces but his mobility comes from a wheelchair.

That wheelchair made sports not only possible but a reality for the otherwise-typical teenager. For years Jeremy begged his mother to let him play soccer. Knowing he couldn't be competitive in soccer on crutches, Angie gently guided him in other directions. When he finally learned to accept the wheelchair, he soon found his niche playing wheelchair basketball and tennis.

Academically, Jeremy is on track with other kids his age. He attends public school in Effingham County at his age/grade level. Math isn't a strong suit, but Angie says that could be more genetics than SB. Because of his hydrocephalus, the Pattersons didn't know if Jeremy would be able to speak. He quickly allayed those fears—talking, communicating and growing up to be a bright young man. One possible effect of Spina Bifida is a lack of organizational skills. Math definitely requires patience and a step-by-step approach to problem-solving, which is Jeremy's weakest point. But, again, Angie's not sure if that's a result of the SB or an inheritance from a left-brained parent.

There are several theories about the cause of Spina Bifida. Some believe there may be a genetic propensity to the birth defect. But most believe it is from a deficiency in folic acid. The spinal cord is one of the first organs to develop—long before many women even know they are pregnant. Angie knew the importance of pre-natal vitamins and tried to take them as recommended. But she had trouble keeping the large pills down and even tried taking children's chewables while trying to get pregnant with Jeremy. She'll never know if the lack of folic acid was the cause of Jeremy's birth defect especially since she had given birth to a healthy Lindsay just two years before. She had the same problem with the vitamins with both her pregnancies.

The challenges of a special needs child were multiplied because of the demands and guilt surrounding her first child. "That was the hardest part, giving birth and needing to stay with him and leaving Lindsay for those first five weeks," says Angie. "And then so much of our life centered around the Spina Bifida. We had to take Jeremy to the doctor every week and to physical therapy. He required so much extra care. We worried we weren't giving Lindsay what she needed."

But that's when the Patterson family philosophy kicked in—to focus on what they can do. For Jeremy, that meant getting him involved in activities like swimming and not regretting that he would probably never play football. Instead of going to water parks, which were inaccessible to Jeremy, they go to the lake where he can swim and enjoy the jet-ski. Lindsay, on the other hand, wanted a trampoline, which would have been torturously off-limits to her brother. So, Angie enrolled Lindsay in gymnastics where she could get her trampoline fix, promoting a skill that enhanced her self-esteem and fostered her independence and development.

When Jeremy was born, the Pattersons lived in Nahunta, Georgia, which is two hours away from Savannah. Shortly after they realized the extent of Jeremy's therapy and treatment needs, they moved to Effingham County to be closer to medical care. Effingham also has an excellent special needs program. All his classes are wheelchair accessible and he's treated like just another kid. "He's had a wonderful attitude. He never felt something was wrong with him. He always thought that since other kids were walking, he could too without his crutches some day," says Angie. "He's stubborn and wants to do stuff and I know he struggles a little and gets frustrated. But overall, he seems okay with it." He took a date to the sixth grade prom, has lots of friends and enjoys his sports. He and his father, Frank, share a love of hunting. And like his fireball of a wife, Frank says they adapt their outings to make them something Jeremy can do, "We build short hunting stands that we can just back a four-wheeler up to and put him in it." And we pick spots where he can move around."

During Jeremy's earlier years, Frank met a man who became his inspiration. When they met, Kenny Collins was older and retired and had a 30-something year old daughter with Spina Bifida. Kenny shared the stories of raising a child before wheelchair ramps and before the American Disabilities Act. In spite of the many social obstacles, the determined father broke through barriers for his child, the hard way. Back then, Kenny was told his child shouldn't go to school because of her condition. So, on weekends, Kenny built wheelchair ramps around the campus using his own money to make sure she had the life she wanted. "When you see somebody else go through something like this without any of the technology and resources we have today, it's inspiring," says Frank. "Kenny Collins was a maverick who forged the way for others."

Over the years, the Pattersons have made life with Spina Bifida seem easy. Lindsay was still a toddler herself when her only sibling was born with his condition. For her, it's simply a way of life. She loves her brother, yet experiences typical teenage angst with him at times. She's never been deprived of anything because of him. Her years in gymnastics taught her discipline and how to focus and accomplish her goals. Frank says she's grown into a wonderful young lady. "I watch her around other people. She's very considerate of others and I think that has a lot to do with Jeremy. She puts other peoples' feelings first. Life is not about her and it never has been. She gets to do things. She enjoys life. I don't think she's ever felt she's been held back, but it has made her grounded and focused."

The Pattersons are grateful that Angie has been able to stay home with both children during their younger years and have put SB in perspective. "We could feel sorry for ourselves (because of Jeremy's condition) but we have met families with children that didn't make it. I only stayed five weeks in the hospital," remembers Angie. "Other families spent months." Frank says both his children give his life purpose. "I'm just another father trying to raise his children. I don't pat myself on the back. God gives you special people and you do what you have to do. Some people think children with handicaps are a burden. We always feel like he's been a blessing."

"There are always tougher situations out there," says Angie. "Somebody else has it worse. Jeremy and I fuss at times but it's a blessing that we can fuss. Some children never get the chance to tell their mother they love them. We focus on what we can do, not what we can't."

## TWO YEARS LATER

Jeremy made it through middle school although each year got a little harder academically. He's fifteen, a sophomore in high school and attends regular classes. Jeremy is still very social and has many friends. He just attended the homecoming dance with a very lovely young lady. Jeremy is very creative and likes to write. There have been a few medical issues that put him in the hospital a few times but he is one tough cookie. His sister, Lindsey, is a senior this year and has been a big help taking him to and from school. This has made them closer and they get along really well. Now that Jeremy has his learner's permit, the plan is for him to take himself to school next year. This will get him one step closer to being independent, which is every parent's dream for their children to grow up and be successful and able to take care of themselves. His mother says she is "not sure what the future has in store for Jeremy but I have no doubt he will do well and have fun doing it."

# Conclusion

With five very busy children and a hectic volunteer schedule, I consider it a miracle this book was ever finished, let alone published. So, if you're not related to me, actually paid for this book and are taking the time to read it, then hallelujah! As I said earlier, *Something Special* Magazine is an incredible tool for reaching out to families, telling their stories and inspiring others. I believe these families' journeys should be shared with people from all over, not just folks in Savannah, Georgia, where we (the editor, writers and photographers) live. That's why I decided to compile this book. I hope it struck a chord with you. After each and every interview, my heart was filled with vast appreciation and gratitude for my own family. My mother always said, "If you have your health, you have everything." Well, I'm sure that's true for some. But, these families who struggle with health, developmental and genetic issues, *still* have EVERYTHING! They have the joy and love that their family members bring them. They have these gifts from God that others may not quite appreciate. They've learned to cherish every moment, every milestone, every breath. I know I hug my own darlings every night a little tighter these days and I'm filled with a greater sense of gratitude for what God has given me. Words cannot express how grateful I am to the parents who were willing to share their very personal stories with me. I am certain I didn't do their situations justice but I pray they know I tried with all my ability. Their courage, strength and devotion are not easy to describe. I hope I was able to at least nick the surface of their sacrifice and infinite capacity to love unconditionally.

If you'd like to know more about *Something Special* Magazine or would like to keep up with the quarterly issues, you can go to www.somethingspecialmagazine.com. There are many more features and testimonials than what you have read in this book. I have shared here only some of the stories in this incredible periodical. I hope you enjoyed this collection and, as our leader/ editor Katrina always says, "I hope you have a blessed day!"